Explore
the Bible.

GENESIS

The Life of Jacob

D1609066

LifeWay Press® • Nashville, Tennessee

Explore the Bible ®

Let the Word dwell in you.

With *Explore the Bible* groups can expect to engage Scripture in its proper context and be better prepared to live it out in their own context. These book-by-book studies will help participants—

> grow in their love for Scripture;

> gain new knowledge about what the Bible teaches;

> develop biblical disciplines;

> internalize the Word in a way that transforms their lives.

Connect

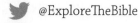

@ExploreTheBible

facebook.com/explorethebible

lifeway.com/explorethebible

ministrygrid.com/web/explorethebible

EXPLORE THE BIBLE:
Genesis—The Life of Jacob

© 2018 LifeWay Press®

ISBN 978-1-5359-4144-0 • Item 005811534

Dewey decimal classification: 221.92
Subject headings: JACOB / GOD—
WILL / BIBLE. O.T.—GENESIS

MICHAEL KELLEY
Director, Groups Ministry

CHUCK KELLEY
General Editor

Send questions/comments to: Content Editor, *Explore the Bible: Small-Group Study;* One LifeWay Plaza; Nashville, TN 37234.

Printed in Canada

For ordering or inquiries visit LifeWay.com; write to LifeWay Small Groups; One LifeWay Plaza; Nashville, TN 37234; or call toll free 800-458-2772.

Quotations by Victor Hugo, Billy Sunday, Augustine of Hippo, John Ortberg, and Kimberly Johnson are taken from Craig Brian Larson and Brian Lowery, gen. eds, *1,001 Quotations That Connect* (Grand Rapids, MI: Zondervan, 2009). Session 2 quotation: Frederick Buechner, as quoted in David L. McKenna, *Christ-Centered Leadership* (Eugene, OR: Cascade, 2013), 41.

CONTENTS

ABOUT THIS STUDY

Genesis, meaning "origins" or "beginnings," receives its title from the first verse, "In the beginning." As both the first book of the Bible and the Pentateuch (the first five books of the Old Testament), Genesis establishes the historical and theological foundation on which many Christian doctrines rest.

In the second section of Genesis, chapters 12–50, the major themes include God's covenant with Abraham, the formation of the nation of Israel and its land, God's promise, and God's blessing. This Bible study will specifically focus on these themes as reflected in the life of Jacob, recorded in Genesis 27–33.

The *Explore the Bible* series will help you know and apply the encouraging, empowering truth of God's Word. Each session is organized in the following way.

UNDERSTAND THE CONTEXT: This page explains the original circumstances and setting of each passage and identifies the primary themes.

EXPLORE THE TEXT: This page introduces the Bible passage, providing helpful commentary and encouraging thoughtful interaction with God through His Word.

APPLY THE TEXT: This page helps you and your group members apply the truths you've explored. It's not enough to know what the Bible says. God's Word has the power to change your life.

DAILY EXPLORATION: Go deeper into God's Word, building on the group experience. Engage in these daily Bible studies, reflect on the questions, record your thoughts, and take action.

OBEY THE TEXT: These pages provide opportunities to obey the Scripture you've studied by responding to questions, memorizing verses, journaling, and praying.

LEADER GUIDE: This final section provides discussion starters and suggested questions to help someone lead a group in reviewing the daily exploration.

GENERAL EDITOR

Chuck Kelley is the president of New Orleans Baptist Theological Seminary. He holds a bachelor of arts from Baylor University and a master of divinity and doctor of theology from New Orleans Baptist Theological Seminary. A much-requested public speaker throughout the Southern Baptist Convention, Dr. Kelley is widely recognized both for his evangelistic preaching and for his research in church growth.

ABOUT GENESIS 27–33

Genesis 12–50 explores the roots of the gospel. Earlier in Genesis God had made a covenant with Abraham. In these chapters the stories of Abraham's descendants unfold. Isaac, Jacob, and their children become the focal points. Sin, brokenness, and jealousy are present in abundance, making the necessity for transformation clear.

In the midst of all this brokenness, God used imperfect people with imperfect lives to advance His perfect plans. Jacob is a perfect example of that divinely orchestrated process. In his story, recorded in Genesis 27–33, we'll see the way God transformed Jacob so completely that he received a new name.

We'll also recognize the role of redemption in God's plan. Jacob's character flaws didn't interrupt God's work but becamse a part of God's redemption story.

Both transformation and redemption are included in the story of every believer. This Bible study will help you better understand your journey of faith. How has faith transformed your life? Like Jacob, do you need even further transformation? Who around you needs the transformation the gospel brings?

Christ came into the world to make transformation and redemption available to all who repent and believe. As you study Genesis 27–33, may God teach you why the gospel is such good news!

For helps on how to use *Explore the Bible*, tips on how to better lead groups, or additional ideas for leading, visit ministrygrid.com/web/explorethebible.

The Deceiver

God accomplishes His purposes despite His covenant people's sin.

Genesis 27:18-29

Please wait behind blue line.
Veuillez patienter derrière la ligne bleue.

What may cause a person to intentionally deceive others? How do you typically respond after you discover that you were deceived?

You view a social-media post that promises a free getaway, noticing that it came from a friend. You click on the image only to discover that the free getaway has some catches. You're required to use a specific airline and a specific booking agency. You also discover additional fees for the "free" trip. You then discover that if you share this post with other people, some fees will be waived. Suddenly you're not nearly as interested in the trip.

❯ UNDERSTAND THE CONTEXT

Abraham died when he was 175 years old, leaving behind two sons, Ishmael and Isaac (see Gen. 25:7-9). Because Ishmael wasn't the promised son (see 17:18-19), Isaac received God's blessings (see 25:11), including the covenant God had made with Abraham (see 12:1-3; 26:1-5). Isaac married Rebekah (see 25:20), and they had twin boys, Esau and Jacob (see 25:24-26). Born only seconds before Jacob, Esau was the oldest and, as a result, first in line for his father's patriarchal blessing. But God selected Jacob instead to be the patriarch (see 25:23). Although the word *patriarch* doesn't appear in the Old Testament, the New Testament uses this descriptive title to refer to Abraham (see Heb. 7:4), the sons of Jacob (see Acts 7:8-9), and David (see Acts 2:29).

Isaac's family was divided by marked favoritism. Isaac favored Esau because, like him, Esau was an outdoorsman, while Rebekah favored Jacob (see Gen. 25:27-28), creating conflict and competition between the two sons. One day when Esau came home exhausted and hungry from hunting, Jacob offered his brother a meal, only after Esau promised him the older brother's birthright (see vv. 29-34).

As Genesis 27 opens, Isaac was old and nearly blind (see vv. 1-2). Before giving Esau the patriarchal blessing, Isaac asked him to hunt some wild game for a meal. Rebekah, who was secretly listening, quickly devised a deceptive plan whereby she cooked a similar meal, dressed Jacob to resemble Esau, and had him steal his brother's blessing (see vv. 3-17). Although the plan was his mother's, Jacob eagerly went along. Because he was ambitious, his only concern was that he might be caught (see vv. 11-12). But when his mother agreed to take his father's wrath (see v. 13), he concluded that the reward outweighed the risk.

❯ GENESIS 27:18-29

18 When he came to his father, he said, "My father." And he answered, "Here I am. Who are you, my son?" **19** Jacob replied to his father, "I am Esau, your **firstborn ❶**. I have done as you told me. Please **sit up ❷** and eat some of my game so that you may bless me." **20** But Isaac said to his son, "How did you ever find it so quickly, my son?" He replied, "Because the LORD your God made it happen for me." **21** Then Isaac said to Jacob, "Please come **closer ❸** so I can touch you, my son. Are you really my son Esau or not?" **22** So Jacob came closer to his father Isaac. When he touched him, he said, "The voice is the voice of Jacob, but the hands are the hands of Esau." **23** He did not recognize him, because his hands were **hairy ❹** like those of his brother Esau; so he blessed him. **24** Again he asked, "Are you really my son Esau?" And he replied, "I am." **25** Then he said, "Bring it closer to me, and let me eat some of my son's game so that I can bless you." Jacob brought it closer to him, and he ate; he brought him wine, and he drank. **26** Then his father Isaac said to him, "Please come closer and kiss me, my son." **27** So he came closer and kissed him. When Isaac smelled his clothes, he blessed him and said: "Ah, the smell of my son is like the smell of a field that the LORD has blessed. **28** May God give to you— from the dew of the sky and from the richness of the land—an abundance of grain and new wine. **29** May peoples serve you and nations bow in worship to you. Be **master ❺** over your relatives; may your mother's sons bow in worship to you. Those who curse you will be cursed, and those who bless you will be blessed."

Passage Outline

A Deceitful Son
(Gen. 27:18-23)

A Deceived Father
(Gen. 27:24-27)

A Stolen Blessing
(Gen. 27:28-29)

Keywords

❶ Jacob and Esau were twins. Esau was born first with Jacob "grasping Esau's heel with his hand" (25:26). God called Israel his "firstborn son" (Ex. 4:22). Jesus is called "the firstborn among many" (Rom. 8:29), "the firstborn over all creation" (Col. 1:15), and "the firstborn from the dead" (Col. 1:18).

❷ Isaac was at least 100 years old, and he lived to be 180 (35:28). Isaac's failing eyesight appears to have made him more aware of his mortality.

❸ This word, used six times in verses 21-27, reveals Isaac's doubt, Jacob's fear of being caught, and the deceptive nature of the entire scene.

❹ Esau had "hair like a fur coat" (25:25).

❺ A fulfillment of the prophecy announced to Rebekah prior to the birth of her sons (Gen. 25:23).

› EXPLORE THE TEXT

Isaac was old, no less than one hundred (see 25:26; 26:34), and believed he was approaching death (see 27:1-2). In Old Testament times a father's blessing was more than an expression of love. The blessing of the father, as the patriarch of the family, was an official, binding transfer of the patriarchal line, along with a prayer for prosperity and superiority. Isaac's blessing also meant the recipient and his descendants would be heirs of the covenant God had originally made with Abraham (see 12:1-3) and extended through Isaac (see 26:1-5).

When Jacob came to his father, posing as Esau, Isaac sensed something was wrong. After lying about his identity, the meal, God's help, and his appearance, Jacob deceived his father.

When dealing with people who don't always act with integrity and transparency, what can believers gain by setting an example?

The kiss was a formal part of giving and receiving a blessing. Here it marked the end of the ceremonial meal (also a formal part of the blessing) and the beginning of the spoken blessing. Isaac's doubts about his son's identity had been removed. How was Isaac so easily deceived? His preferential love for the older son led to his deception. He heard (see 27:24), tasted (see v. 25), touched (see v. 26), and smelled (see v. 27) what he was looking for—Esau. Because of his unrelenting favoritism, he believed because he wanted to believe.

What are some ways favoritism is manifested in the church? What are some consequences that result from favoritism? How can we prevent it?

Through an act of deception, the blessing went to Jacob. Although Jacob took what God had promised him (see 25:23), this deception wasn't God's doing. We can't justify using deceptive means to obtain worthy ends.

In spite of Jacob's deplorable actions, God was faithful to His promise. God's promises are immutable, that is, unchangeable, based on His divine wisdom. They don't rely on our actions but on His absolute faithfulness. Although Jacob's life journey could have been more enjoyable if he had waited on the Lord, God delivered on His promise, as He always does. Because Jacob did things his own way, God sent him to the school of hard knocks. Along the way God broke Jacob's selfishness and transformed him into a man He could bless.

What are some occasions in Scripture when God accomplished His purposes despite a person's sinful conduct? What can we learn about God from those examples?

> BIBLE SKILL: **Use other Scriptures to better understand a Bible passage.** ›>
> In Genesis 27:29 Isaac quoted from God's original call of Abraham in Genesis 12:1-3. Read Genesis 13:14-16; 15:1-6; 17:1-8,19; 22:15-18; 26:2-5; 35:9-12. What lines from the original passage are repeated in these verses? What statements are added to the original? How does Christ fit into this promise?

› APPLY THE TEXT

> › Believers are to act with integrity and transparency when dealing with others.

> › Believers must guard against favoritism, knowing it leads to personal deception.

> › God can bring to pass His sovereign purpose despite the selfish actions of a sinful person.

Rate your integrity and transparency on a scale of 1 to 10, with 1 being never and 10 being always. What steps do you need to take to more consistently show integrity and transparency?

What steps are you taking to avoid showing favoritism? What Bible passages are you memorizing to remind yourself not to show favoritism?

How can your group help others determine whether their actions are selfish? How can your group encourage people to faithfully follow God's sovereign purpose?

❯ DAILY EXPLORATION

Day 1: It's tempting to deceive others.

Read Genesis 27:18-20, looking for ways Jacob deceived Isaac.

When Jacob came to his father, posing as Esau, Isaac sensed something was wrong. He questioned Jacob four times in verses 18-24. With each question Jacob could have revealed his true identity and ended the ruse, but each time, without hesitation, he answered with a lie.

Motivated by greed, Jacob deliberately lied to his father. This wasn't the first lie a patriarch had told. Jacob's grandfather, Abraham, had lied when he claimed that Sarah wasn't his wife (see 12:11-13), and his father, Isaac, had lied about Rebekah (see 26:7). Whenever lying becomes a way of life, it easily passes from one generation to the next. When Jacob told the first lie, it became easier to lie again. The same is true for believers today.

Isaac seemed to be suspicious. Jacob then brought God into the conversation. Notice that Jacob referred to Yahweh as Isaac's God, not his own. This was the first time either the father or the son mentioned God in the entire chapter, and Jacob blasphemously used His name to cover a lie.

What are some situations in which you might be tempted to deceive another person? How can you maintain your integrity in these situations?

Day 2: Be an example.

Read Genesis 27:21-24, considering Isaac's confusion.

Requesting Jacob to come closer indicated Isaac's growing suspicion. Wearing Esau's garments (see v. 15), Jacob smelled like Esau, but his voice still sounded like Jacob. Isaac believed that if he could touch his arms, he could determine his true identity because Esau was hairy and Jacob had smooth skin (see v. 11). Thinking ahead, Rebekah had taken the skin of goats and fashioned it into two tight wrappings that covered Jacob's forearms (see v. 16).

After lying about his identity, the meal, God's help, and his appearance, Jacob deceived his father. However, the taste of victory is never as sweet when taken by deceit. Jacob had numerous opportunities to stop the lies. His calloused heart caused him to seek only the end, but as we'll see, it wasn't the end he expected.

Often we want our Bible heroes to be flawless. But we must remember that no one has been or is perfect except Jesus. Only by the Lord's grace and our commitment to integrity and transparency when dealing with others can we reach our godly potential.

When dealing with people who don't always act with integrity and transparency, what can you gain by setting an example?

Day 3: Avoid favoritism.

Read Genesis 27:25-27, paying close attention to verse 27.

Isaac instructed Jacob to bring the meal closer to him, indicating that he was ready to eat. Isaac's doubts about his son's identity were removed when he smelled Jacob. Isaac now seemed convinced that this was Esau.

How was Isaac so easily deceived? His preferential love for the older son led to his deception. He heard (see 27:24), tasted (see v. 25), touched (see v. 26), and smelled (see v. 27) what he was looking for—Esau. Because of his unrelenting favoritism, he believed because he wanted to believe.

Children should honor their parents, and parents should also love their children equally, training them in the ways of the Lord without favoritism (see Eph. 6:4). Believers must also guard against favoritism in the church. The Bible repeatedly warns against showing favoritism (see 1 Tim. 5:21; Jas. 2:1). Because Christ died for all, all believers have equal value before God (see Gal. 3:28).

What are some consequences that result from favoritism? How can you avoid showing favoritism in your family?

KEY DOCTRINE: **Family** >> Parents are to teach their children spiritual and moral values and to lead them, through consistent lifestyle example and loving discipline, to make choices based on biblical truth (see Deut. 6:4-9).

Day 4: The end doesn't justify the means.

Read Genesis 27:28-29, noting the blessing Isaac gave Jacob.

Finishing what he started in verse 23, Isaac blessed the wrong son. Most official announcements are dispatched in a monotone voice, void of passion. But handing the torch to the man he thought was Esau was surely different for Isaac. This blessing would forever change his son's destiny. Emotionally charged, he painted a beautiful future for his son, using the words *you* and *your* eight times in these two verses. Specifically, Isaac asked God to bless his son in four areas: prosperity, power, prominence, and protection.

But the blessing didn't go to Esau. In an act of deception, it went to Jacob. Although Jacob took what God had promised him (see 25:23), this deception wasn't God's doing. We can't justify using deceptive means to obtain worthy ends. Jacob orchestrated these events. Because Jacob stole the blessing, it cost him dearly.

Did receiving the blessing justify the means of Jacob's deception? Explain.

Day 5: God's plan will prevail.

Read Genesis 27:18-29, reviewing the depth of Jacob's deception.

What are the consequences of getting ahead of God?

1. Jacob's brother was so angry that he determined to kill Jacob (see 27:41).

2. Jacob had to flee for his life (see 27:43).

3. Jacob's uncle, Laban, deceived him into working fourteen years for his wife Rachel (see 29:20,30).

4. Jacob's brother would become the founder of an enemy nation (see 32:3; 1 Sam. 14:47-48).

5. Jacob would be separated from his family for twenty-one years (see Gen. 33:1-4).

6. Jacob never saw his mother again (see 49:31).

Imagine how different life would have been if Jacob had waited for God to work His way in His time. God, always faithful to His Word, prepares His people to receive His promises. If we respond in a sinful way, God can bring to pass His sovereign purposes despite our selfish actions. Let Jacob's misery remind you to faithfully follow God, even when you don't understand how He can bring His plan to fruition.

What are some occasions in Scripture when God accomplished His purposes despite a person's sinful conduct? What can we learn about God from those examples?

To lie a little is not possible;
whoever lies, lies a whole lie.

VICTOR HUGO

❯ OBEY THE TEXT

Reflect on the truths found in Genesis 27 and record your responses to the following questions or discuss them with two other members of your Bible-study group.

In what ways did Jacob take advantage of his father? Consider a time when you took advantage of a situation. Was that action beneficial to you in the long run? Why or why not?

How did Isaac's and Rebekah's favoritism with their sons affect their family? What examples of favoritism have you seen in your family?

In what areas of your life can you show integrity and trust in the Lord this week?

MEMORIZE

The LORD said to her: Two nations are in your womb;
two peoples will come from you and be separated.
One people will be stronger than the other,
and the older will serve the younger.
GENESIS 25:23

MY THOUGHTS

Record insights and questions from this session's group experience
and daily exploration.

_____

_____

_____

_____

_____

_____

_____

MY RESPONSE

Note specific ways you'll put into practice the truth explored this week.

_____

_____

_____

_____

_____

_____

_____

_____

MY PRAYERS

List specific prayer needs and answers to remember this week.

_____

_____

_____

_____

_____

_____

_____

_____

Not Alone

God reveals His purpose to the people He chooses.

Genesis 28:10-22

What situations or experiences may make a person feel alone? What other factors contribute to a person's feeling of loneliness?

Loneliness is more than location. We can be in a familiar place yet still be alone. We may be sitting in our apartment or house, surrounded by objects that are important to us, and still feel alone. We can feel equally alone in a room full of people or walking down a city street surrounded by a mass of people. The feeling of aloneness can be overwhelming.

❯ UNDERSTAND **THE CONTEXT**

After learning that he had been tricked into giving the patriarchal blessing to Jacob, Isaac trembled uncontrollably (see Gen. 27:33). He shook with fear, not only because he hadn't blessed his favored son, Esau, but also because the blessing was irrevocable. Everything, including the Abrahamic covenant, now belonged to Jacob (see v. 37).

With a loud, bitter cry Esau begged his father for a blessing (see v. 34), but the only blessing Isaac could give him was dreadful in comparison (see vv. 38-40). His land wouldn't be fruitful like Jacob's. Instead of ruling over nations and his family with divine protection, Esau would live a life consisting of warfare and servitude. Filled with rage, Esau vowed that he would kill his twin after a proper time of mourning after their father had died (see v. 41). However, Isaac would live many more years, dying at the age of 180 (see 35:28).

Fearing that her angry son would act on his threat, Rebekah quickly devised a twofold plan to ensure Jacob's safety.

1. She instructed Jacob to go to her brother, Laban, and stay with him for a few days (see 27:42-44). Thinking Esau's wrath would be short-lived, she promised Jacob that she would send for him when things settled down (see v. 45).

2. Rebekah told Isaac that Esau's foreign wives were making life miserable for her. Using the guise that she couldn't bear the same fate when Jacob married, she convinced Isaac to send Jacob to her brother's family for a wife (see 27:46–28:1). Isaac agreed, sending Jacob with his blessing (see 28:2-5).

The only problem with Rebekah's plan was that Jacob's trip didn't last a few days but twenty-one years (see 33:1-4). Little did she know that she would never see her favorite son again; she died before Jacob could return home (see 49:31). While Jacob was on the run, his life took an unexpected turn before he reached Haran. He met God.

GENESIS 28:10-22

10 Jacob left **Beer-sheba** Ⓐ and went toward Haran. **11** He reached a certain place and spent the night there because the sun had set. He took one of the stones from the place, put it there at his head, and lay down in that place. **12** And he **dreamed** Ⓑ: A stairway was set on the ground with its top reaching the sky, and God's angels were going up and down on it. **13** The LORD was standing there beside him, saying, "I am the LORD, the God of your father Abraham and the God of Isaac. I will give you and your offspring the land on which you are lying. **14** Your offspring will be like the dust of the earth, and you will spread out toward the west, the east, the north, and the south. All the peoples on earth will be **blessed through you** Ⓒ and your offspring. **15** Look, I am with you and will watch over you wherever you go. I will bring you back to this land, for I will not leave you until I have done what I have promised you." **16** When Jacob awoke from his sleep, he said, "Surely the LORD is in this place, and I did not know it." **17** He was afraid and said, "What an awesome place this is! This is none other than the **house of God** Ⓓ. This is the gate of heaven." **18** Early in the morning Jacob took the stone that was near his head and set it up as a marker. He poured oil on top of it **19** and named the place Bethel, though previously the city was named Luz. **20** Then Jacob made a vow: "If God will be with me and watch over me during this journey I'm making, if he provides me with food to eat and clothing to wear, **21** and if I return safely to my father's family, then the LORD will be my God. **22** This stone that I have set up as a marker will be God's house, and I will give to you a tenth of all that you give me."

Passage Outline

Purpose Revealed
(Gen. 28:10-15)

Presence Realized
(Gen. 28:16-19)

Commitment Made
(Gen. 28:20-22)

Keywords

Ⓐ An important location for Jacob's family. There Abraham had dug a well, planted a tamarisk tree, and "called on … God" (Gen. 21:33). The Lord had appeared to Isaac there.

Ⓑ Dreams were one of many ways God spoke to people in biblical times. Jacob's son Joseph is well known for his dreams.

Ⓒ This phrase was first stated to Abraham, then to Isaac, and here to Jacob. This aspect of the gospel was proclaimed "ahead of time to Abraham" (Gal. 3:8) and was preached by Peter in Acts 3:25-26, pointing to Jesus as the fulfillment.

Ⓓ This is the first use of this term in the Bible. Later it would be used of the tabernacle, the temple, and the New Testament church.

❯ EXPLORE THE TEXT

Leaving behind his worried mother, angry brother, and deceived father, Jacob left Beer-sheba and set out for Haran, the home of his mother's brother (see Gen. 27:43).

In this solitary place sleep overtook Jacob, and he dreamed. Dreams were one way God delivered His message. In his dream Jacob saw a stairway that reached from earth to heaven. The stairway reminds us of God's personal involvement in the affairs of earth and in the hearts of humanity. Although people like Jacob may leave God out of their lives, God never deserts them.

How can believers be more aware of God's invisible activity around them? Why is it easy to take such activity for granted?

As far as Scripture reveals, this was Jacob's first encounter with God. God extended to Jacob the covenant He had made with Abraham and Isaac (see Gen. 12:1-3; 13:14-17; 26:3-5), promising him offspring, land, blessing through him, divine protection and presence, and safe return home.

What's the connection between God's presence and His promises? How does His promised presence give us hope and strength?

> BIBLE SKILL: **Notice the repetition of phrases in different Bible passages in order to understand their relationship to one another.** >> Read Genesis 12:1-3; 13:14-17; 15:1-7; 17:3-8; 26:3-5; 28:13-15. Make a chart showing repeated phrases and in which verses they occur. What does your chart show you about God's promises to the patriarchs?

Lying down in a lonely, desolate place, Jacob woke up realizing he was never alone. He was afraid, knowing he was in the presence of Holy God. Jacob realized the occasion should be memorialized, so he took the stone that had been his pillow, set it up as a marker, and consecrated it by pouring oil on top of it. This place was previously named Luz, meaning "almond tree." Now it would be known as Bethel, meaning "house of God," for this was the place where Jacob met God. Although Jacob was still far from perfect, his life changed at Bethel for the better.

Why is it important to commemorate God's past blessings? What happens when believers fail to remember His blessings?

To demonstrate his commitment to God, Jacob made a vow. As a result of God's goodness, Jacob declared that the Lord would be his God forever. Jacob's vow was an expression of trust, not in deceptive plans but in God alone. As another demonstration of his new commitment, Jacob promised to give God a tenth of all God had given him.

What do our spiritual commitments reveal about our understanding of God?

› APPLY **THE TEXT**

> › Believers can be confident that God is with them, guiding them to fulfill His purposes for them.

> › Believers can joyfully and gratefully commemorate God's work in their lives.

> › Believers are to take steps of faith in response when God speaks to them.

Reflect on Genesis 28:15. Write the verse on a card, refer to it throughout this week, and try to memorize it. How can the truth of this passage help you face a current challenge?

List your spiritual milestones and record where they took place. Thank God for working in your life and for never leaving you. Share with one person this week some ways God has worked and is working in your life.

How can your group encourage other people to take steps of faith? As the first step, consider using the personal testimonies of people who've already responded to God by faith. What other steps can your group use?

THIS WAY

❯ DAILY EXPLORATION

Day 1: Sin has consequences.

Read Genesis 28:10-11, considering how Jacob might have felt on his journey.

Jacob left Beer-sheba and set out for Haran. When the sun had set, he stopped to rest at "a certain place" (v. 11). The word *place* appears six times in this account (see vv. 11,16-17,19). This place was far from home, far away from his mother's tender touch, and far away from the luxuries afforded him as Isaac's son. In this place, alone, he had no need for deception or trickery. Most likely his thoughts were now filled with fear. *Would Esau follow him and kill him? Would he have enough food or water? Would he find his way to Haran? Would his uncle welcome him under these circumstances?* His deceptive actions brought him to this uninviting, uncomfortable place with only a stone for a pillow.

The consequences of our sinful actions often take us to places we didn't imagine. We fantasize about riches and fame, but sin offers no such reward (see Jas. 1:14-15). Like Jacob, we may find ourselves without family and home if we yield to Satan's temptations.

How have you experienced separation because of your sins? How does that separation help you understand the seriousness of sin?

Day 2: God is all-knowing.

Read Genesis 28:12, noting the details of Jacob's dream.

In his dream Jacob saw a stairway that reached from earth to heaven. God's angels were going up and down on it. Angels are divine messengers who carry out God's will as He directs them. These messengers travel between heaven and earth and operate equally in both realms.

Notice the movement of the angels on the stairway. They were already on earth, traveling up to heaven and then coming back down to earth again. God's angelic army had been busy on earth, long before Jacob's time. Not only were the angels accomplishing God's purposes on earth, but by ascending the stairway, they were also in constant communication with heaven. Nothing on earth escapes the watchful eye of God. Even in this solitary place Jacob learned that God was at work.

How can you be more aware of God's invisible activity around you? Why is it easy to take such activity for granted?

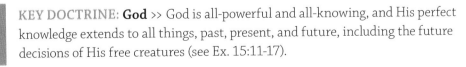

KEY DOCTRINE: **God** >> God is all-powerful and all-knowing, and His perfect knowledge extends to all things, past, present, and future, including the future decisions of His free creatures (see Ex. 15:11-17).

Day 3: God is at work in our lives.

Read Genesis 28:13-15, identifying God's promise to Jacob.

As far as Scripture reveals, this was Jacob's first encounter with God. Introducing Himself, God used the name Yahweh, the personal name for God, meaning the self-existent, eternal God (see Ex. 3:15). The Book of Genesis, as well as the entire Bible, is a revelation of God, showing us who He is and how He deals with people. Just as God appeared to Jacob's grandfather and father, He personally appeared to Jacob. Jacob was about to learn that hearing stories about God wasn't the same as having a personal relationship with Him.

God extended to Jacob the covenant He had made with Abraham and Isaac (see Gen. 12:1-3; 13:14-17; 26:3-5), promising him offspring, land, blessing through him, divine protection and presence, and safe return home. God would appear to Jacob several more times, but this first meeting was significant because Jacob learned that God was interested in him and was at work in his life.

Just as God approached sinful Jacob, Jesus comes to us in spite of our sinfulness. He loves us as we are and blesses us even though we're undeserving. When we place our faith in Jesus, our lives will never be the same. We can be confident that God is with us and guides us to fulfill His purposes in and through us.

How does God's promised presence give you hope and strength?

Day 4: Believers should record significant events with God.

Read Genesis 28:16-19, paying close attention to the way Jacob memorialized the site.

Regardless of how far we run, God is already there waiting for us. Just as He met with Jacob, the Lord longs for an intimate meeting with us. Jacob was afraid, knowing he was in the presence of Holy God. But he was also in awe of the reality that the God of heaven would meet with someone like him. Awareness of being in the Lord's presence often elicits a response like Jacob's. Jacob realized the occasion should be memorialized.

Too often we don't record our significant events with God, forgetting when and where they occurred. What are the pillars in the lives of believers? Salvation, baptism, church membership, answering His call—these are only a few of the events worth remembering and celebrating. Believers everywhere can joyfully and gratefully commemorate God's work in their lives.

What are some appropriate ways you can celebrate God's work in your life?

Day 5: Believers must make a commitment to God.

Read Genesis 28:20-22, highlighting Jacob's commitment.

God demonstrates His commitment in tangible ways. In turn, our commitment to God should be just as tangible as Jacob's was. Jacob first recounted the blessings God gave to him: His presence, protection, provision, and promise of a safe journey home. Jacob wasn't bargaining with God, as if buying His favor; rather, he offered God his vow in confidence of God's promise.

As a result of God's goodness, Jacob declared the Lord would be his God forever. Jacob's vow was an expression of trust, not in deceptive plans but in God alone. Faith has always been a prerequisite for coming to God. Real change manifests itself in visible ways. The proof for Jacob was his tithe. Jacob promised to give back to God, even before the tithe was commanded, as his grandfather, Abraham, had done earlier (see 14:20).

What's the relationship between being and doing in your spiritual life? How do your actions demonstrate who you are and what you believe?

The place God calls you to is the place where your deep gladness and the world's deep hunger meet.

FREDERICK BUECHNER

❯ OBEY THE TEXT

Reflect on the truths found in Genesis 28 and record your responses to the following questions or discuss them with two other members of your Bible-study group.

What was so important about God's promises to Jacob in verse 15? How do those promises apply to your life?

What was Jacob's response to the realization that he had been in the presence of the Lord? What should your response be?

Describe a turning point in your life that resulted from an encounter with the Lord.

MEMORIZE

Look, I am with you and will watch over you wherever you go. I will bring you back to this land, for I will not leave you until I have done what I have promised you.

GENESIS 28:15

MY THOUGHTS

Record insights and questions from this session's group experience
and daily exploration.

MY RESPONSE

Note specific ways you'll put into practice the truth explored this week.

MY PRAYERS

List specific prayer needs and answers to remember this week.

Family

God uses imperfect people with imperfect lives to advance His plans.

Genesis 29:16-30

What are some excuses believers give for not taking an active role in Christian service? How could these excuses point to a faulty understanding of God?

Most of us are aware of our failures and shortcomings. Often this awareness makes us feel disqualified from taking a more active role in Christian service. However, God uses imperfect people to advance His plans. He provides us with the resources required to accomplish any assignment He gives us.

❯ UNDERSTAND THE CONTEXT

Fortified by his experience at Bethel (see Gen. 28:10-22), Jacob pressed on toward his mother's homeland, arriving at a well (see 29:1-2). Water wells were communal places in ancient times. They not only provided drinkable water for people and animals but also afforded opportunities for fellowship, conversation, commerce, and even matchmaking. For example, Abraham's servant found Rebekah as a wife for Isaac at a well (see 24:10-27).

Often what people call chance encounters are divine orchestrations. Arriving at a well where shepherds spoke his language was no accident for Jacob (see 29:3-5). Just as God had met with him at Bethel, God directed him to the family who would help him fulfill the patriarchal covenant (see 28:13-15). Following in the footsteps of his father, Jacob also met his future wife at the well.

At the well Jacob showed signs of a changed life. Instead of taking advantage of the shepherds, he oversaw the watering of the flocks of sheep (see 29:10). Unlike the unfaithful kiss he gave his father (see 27:26-27), Jacob wept as he introduced himself and kissed Rachel (see 29:11-12). After meeting his uncle, Laban, Jacob revealed his life story (see v. 13). He even worked a month without pay for his uncle (see v. 14). Jacob, the former deceiver, was a reformed man. His encounter with God had transformed his life. By turning from lies and deception, Jacob was finally in a position in which God could mold him into a man who was worthy of His covenant.

Having only daughters at that time, Laban gladly welcomed Jacob into his family (see v. 14). After a month of hard work, Laban asked Jacob to name his salary (see v. 15). Jacob responded with a surprising answer: he wanted Laban's daughter Rachel for his wife. Little did Jacob know that the former deceiver had just met his match in Laban.

❯ GENESIS 29:16-30

16 Now Laban had two daughters: the older was named Leah, and the younger was named Rachel. **17** Leah had tender eyes, but Rachel was shapely and beautiful. **18** Jacob loved Rachel, so he answered Laban, "I'll work for you seven years for your younger daughter Rachel." **19** Laban replied, "Better that **I give her to you** Ⓐ than to some other man. Stay with me." **20** So Jacob worked seven years for Rachel, and they seemed like only a few days to him because of his love for her. **21** Then Jacob said to Laban, "Since my time is complete, give me **my wife** Ⓑ, so I can sleep with her." **22** So Laban invited all the men of the place and sponsored a **feast** Ⓒ. **23** That evening, Laban took his daughter Leah and gave her to Jacob, and he slept with her. **24** And Laban gave his slave Zilpah to his daughter Leah as her slave. **25** When morning came, there was Leah! So he said to Laban, "What is this you have done to me? Wasn't it for Rachel that I **worked** Ⓓ for you? Why have you **deceived** Ⓔ me?" **26** Laban answered, "It is not the custom in this place to give the younger daughter in marriage before the firstborn. **27** Complete this week of wedding celebration, and we will also give you this younger one in return for working yet another seven years for me." **28** And Jacob did just that. He finished the week of celebration, and Laban gave him his daughter Rachel as his wife. **29** And Laban gave his slave Bilhah to his daughter Rachel as her slave. **30** Jacob slept with Rachel also, and indeed, he **loved Rachel more** Ⓕ than Leah. And he worked for Laban another seven years.

Passage Outline

Jacob's Proposal
(Gen. 29:16-20)

Laban's Deception
(Gen. 29:21-24)

Seven More Years
(Gen. 29:25-30)

Keywords

Ⓐ Laban was responsible for and protective of his family. Thousands of years later, "Who gives this woman to be married to this man?" is still our custom.

Ⓑ Jacob clearly believed Rachel now belonged to him and with him.

Ⓒ The New Testament uses the wedding feast as a picture of believers celebrating with Jesus in heaven (Matt. 22:1-14; 25:1-13; Rev. 19:6-9).

Ⓓ Laban took full advantage of Jacob's work ethic.

Ⓔ Jacob had been a deceiver of others (Gen. 27:19,36); now he had been deceived.

Ⓕ Favoritism was a common, destructive problem for the patriarchs and their families. For example, Abraham favored Isaac, Isaac favored Esau, and Rebekah favored Jacob.

❯ EXPLORE THE TEXT

Sent to Haran by his parents in hopes that he would find a wife, Jacob found more than a wife. He learned the value of putting people he loved above himself, along with the value of working for what he wanted instead of using deception.

Rachel's appearance might have attracted Jacob, but he wasn't motivated by lust, a fact demonstrated by his willingness to work for her hand in marriage. Proving his love and desiring a dowry worthy of his love for Rachel, Jacob offered his uncle seven years of labor.

What can we learn from Jacob's example of purposeful work? How can we find purpose in our work, regardless of its nature?

A casual reader might conclude that Jacob asked Laban for Rachel to be his wife, but Jacob actually said, "Give me my wife" (v. 21). Scripture doesn't record Jacob's asking for Rachel by name, although if taken in context with the previous verses, Jacob's request was clear. By being unclear, however, he left himself open to deception.

After the whole community enjoyed the wedding feast, Laban substituted Leah for Rachel. In exchange for her part in the hoax, Leah received a personal servant. Leah could easily have revealed the plot, but that action would have had other consequences.

What may keep people from speaking up when they become aware of a deceptive act? Do any of these reasons excuse them from responsibility? Explain.

The deceiver was now the deceived. Anguish poured from Jacob's heart as he pleaded with Laban. Laban never explained why he intentionally misled Jacob. His only response was an appeal to local custom (see v. 26).

Weddings in the Old Testament consisted of weeklong celebrations. In return for Jacob's promise not to spoil the celebration, Laban promised Jacob that he could marry Rachel for another seven years of labor. From this ordeal Jacob matured, learning the value of submission to those in authority over him and to God's plan for his life.

Why is maintaining a godly perspective in challenging times important for believers? How can believers maintain a godly perspective?

> **BIBLE SKILL: Use other Scriptures to better understand an attribute of God. >>**
> Scan the Book of Jonah, looking for his imperfections. How do Jonah's shortcomings compare to Jacob's? What can we learn about God's grace? What can we learn about what qualifies a person to be used by God?

❯ APPLY THE TEXT

> ❯ Joy can be found in purposeful work.

> ❯ Believers should take seriously the fact that in God's economy, people reap the attitudes and actions they sow.

> ❯ Believers can thank God for His faithfulness to His promises even when our plans are contrary to His wise design.

Discuss a type of ministry your group could do in your community. How could you use that work to demonstrate Christ to others? What steps does the group need to take in order to commit to a work project that benefits your community?

Examine your attitudes. How do they affect your actions? How do your attitudes need to change?

List ways God is using you to make a difference for His kingdom. Take time to thank Him for using you. Make yourself available for Him to use you as He desires.

❯ DAILY EXPLORATION

Day 1: Joy can be found in purposeful work.

Read Genesis 29:16-20, considering Jacob's intentions.

In ancient times a prospective suitor offered a dowry as compensation or reimbursement for the loss of a daughter. Unlike his grandfather, Abraham, who handsomely paid for his mother, Rebekah (see 24:50-53), Jacob had nothing of value. Because Rachel was a shepherdess for her father (see 29:6), Laban's economic loss would be substantial. Proving his love and desiring a dowry worthy of his love for Rachel, Jacob offered his uncle seven years of labor.

Although shepherding wasn't an easy vocation, Jacob patiently worked seven years for his goal. That's a radical departure for a young man who had rushed ahead of God's timing when he stole his brother's blessing (see 27:33-35). Because Jacob was motivated by love for Rachel, those years must have seemed only a few days to him. Genuine love makes any sacrifice and pays any cost.

Working and waiting for Rachel's hand in marriage filled Jacob with joy. Joy can be found in purposeful work. Meaningful work, no matter how mundane, can make time pass swiftly and, most of all, can make life worth living.

How can you find purpose in your work, regardless of its nature?

Day 2: Deception causes pain.

Read Genesis 29:21-24, noting Laban's deception.

Jacob fully completed his part of the bargain for Rachel. He was a man of his word, showing a departure from his previous lifestyle. Yet unknown to him at the time, a price remained to be paid. The man who had deceived his father had now been deceived by his father-in-law. Experiencing the principle of sowing and reaping, Jacob would soon understand the pain his own deception had caused his father and his brother.

Several questions arise about Leah. Was she a willing partner in her father's subterfuge, or did he force her into submission? Where was Rachel during the wedding? Could she have intervened? Had this been Laban's plan all along? The abrupt mention of the father's wedding gift might offer a clue. In exchange for her part in the hoax, Leah received a personal servant. Leah could easily have revealed the plot, but that would have embarrassed her father before his guests, a cultural taboo. Moreover, such an action could have had other consequences. Jacob could have been banished without Rachel, leaving Leah to live with a disappointed sister and an angry father.

What keeps you from speaking up when you become aware of a deceptive act?
Do any of these reasons excuse you from responsibility? Explain.

Day 3: Believers must maintain a godly perspective during challenging times.

Read Genesis 29:25-26, identifying the local custom Laban mentioned.

Jacob's three questions reveal much about his emotional state at that moment. With the first question Jacob expressed disbelief. The second question revealed his anger. His final question indicated resignation or acceptance of his situation. As a man who had deceived his way through life, eating the bitter fruit of deception wasn't a pleasant experience.

Laban never explained why he intentionally misled Jacob. His only response was an appeal to local custom. Before the ceremony Laban could have pulled Jacob aside and broken the news, but he didn't. Jacob had repeatedly demonstrated his disregard for family customs earlier in his life. By taking advantage of his brother, he had usurped the birthright tradition, and by taking advantage of his father's frailties, he had stolen the traditional blessing. Unfazed by family customs, Jacob was now forced to respect family practices. Although not all family traditions are healthy or scriptural, respect is a key characteristic of every home.

Why is maintaining a godly perspective in challenging times important for you?

Day 4: God is faithful to His promises.

Read Genesis 29:27-30, looking for ways God would fulfill His promises to Jacob through the situation.

From this ordeal Jacob matured, learning the value of submission to those in authority over him and to God's plan for his life. What about poor Leah? God saw that Jacob didn't love her as much as her sister, so He had compassion on her, giving her the privilege of bearing Jacob his first four sons (see vv. 32-35), who would love her, reminding us that God hears the cries of our broken hearts.

Laban no doubt thought he was the ultimate winner. Little did he know that God was using him to fulfill His promise to make Jacob's offspring as numerous as the dust of the earth (see 28:14). From Jacob's two wives and their handmaidens would come twelve sons who would become the twelve tribes of Israel (see 29:31–30:24), fulfilling the promised covenant God had made with Abraham. Regardless of where life takes you, you can rest assured that God will be faithful to His promises.

How have God's plans for you been different from what you had planned for your life?

Day 5: God has an intended design for marriage.

Read Genesis 29:16-30, reviewing the lessons learned in this passage.

God's design for marriage is one man and one woman, evidenced by Adam and Eve and reinforced by the teachings of the New Testament (see Eph. 5:22-33; 1 Pet. 3:1-7). Never confuse human plans with God's purpose and never confuse His permissiveness with His approval.

 KEY DOCTRINE: The family >> Marriage is the uniting of one man and one woman in covenant commitment for a lifetime (see Gen. 1:26-28).

What do you see as the consequences of unions outside God's intended design for marriage?

I sometimes wonder whether the church needs new members one-half as much as she needs the old bunch made over.

BILLY SUNDAY

❯ OBEY THE TEXT

Reflect on the truths found in Genesis 29 and record your responses to the following questions or discuss them with two other members of your Bible-study group.

The old saying is true, but why does time fly when you're having fun?

How might Leah have felt about her role in the situation? How have you felt in situations when someone was being deceived?

When have you seen God work through complicated circumstances to bring blessings and fulfill His purposes?

MEMORIZE

She conceived again, gave birth to a son, and said, "This time I will praise the LORD." Therefore she named him Judah. Then Leah stopped having children.

GENESIS 29:35

MY THOUGHTS

Record insights and questions from this session's group experience and daily exploration.

MY RESPONSE

Note specific ways you'll put into practice the truth explored this week.

MY PRAYERS

List specific prayer needs and answers to remember this week.

Home

God is with His people, giving direction for living.

Genesis 31:2-16

What makes a place feel like home? What makes the longing for home such a strong emotion?

Nothing stirs our hearts like a longing for home, especially if we've been away for an extended time. For most of us, home holds fond memories of love, acceptance, faith, and laughter. It's also the place we turn to when we need rest and direction. There really is no place like home.

❯ UNDERSTAND **THE CONTEXT**

With two wives, two maidservants, eleven sons, and a daughter, Jacob longed for home after working fourteen years for Laban (see Gen. 30:25). Jacob's large family came from his two wives, Leah and Rachel, and their two servants, Zilpah and Bilhah. Leah's children included Reuben, Simeon, Levi, Judah (see 29:31-35), Issachar, Zebulun, and Dinah (see 30:17-21). Rachel's sons were Joseph and Benjamin (see 30:22-24; 35:16-18). Bilhah, Rachel's maid, bore Dan and Naphtali (see 30:1-8). Jacob's sons through Zilpah, Leah's maid, were Gad and Asher (see vv. 9-13).

Jacob wasn't just homesick. Lodged deep in his heart was the promise God had given him earlier at Bethel: a bright, secure future in Canaan (see 28:13-15). As the years passed, Jacob yearned for home and for the fulfillment of those blessings. Reminding Laban of how hard he had worked, Jacob pleaded for an unconditional release from his father-in-law's control (see 30:26).

Jacob proposed to Laban a deal that on the surface favored Laban (see vv. 29-34). In those days sheep were predominately white, while goats were black. Jacob would continue shepherding Laban's flocks, but any sheep or goats that were mixed in color would be Jacob's personal flock. Thinking he had the upper hand, Laban quickly agreed. He even separated the mixed-colored animals and gave them to his sons for shepherding, moving them a three-day journey from Jacob and the rest of the flock (see vv. 35-36).

Because of God's hand on his life, Jacob bred a large herd that was discolored, making him wealthy after just six years (see 30:37-43; 31:38). Realizing Laban wouldn't release him, especially with all of his wealth, Jacob planned his exit strategy. Before he could put his plan into motion, he needed the support of his family. In a place far from Laban, Jacob gathered his family and poured out his heart by sharing God's vision for their lives.

GENESIS 31:2-16

2 Jacob saw from Laban's **face** Ⓐ that his attitude toward him was not the same as before. **3** The LORD said to him, "Go back to the **land of your fathers** Ⓑ and to your family, and **I will be with you** Ⓒ."
4 Jacob had Rachel and Leah called to the field where his flocks were. **5** He said to them, "I can see from your father's face that his attitude toward me is not the same as before, but the God of my father has been with me. **6** You know that with all my strength I have served your father **7** and that he has cheated me and changed my wages ten times. **But God** Ⓓ has not let him harm me. **8** If he said, 'The spotted sheep will be your wages,' then all the sheep were born spotted. If he said, 'The streaked sheep will be your wages,' then all the sheep were born streaked. **9** God has taken away your father's herds and given them to me. **10** When the flocks were breeding, **I saw in a dream** Ⓔ that the streaked, spotted, and speckled males were mating with the females. **11** In that dream the angel of God said to me, 'Jacob!' and I said, 'Here I am.' **12** And he said, 'Look up and see: all the males that are mating with the flocks are streaked, spotted, and speckled, for I have seen all that Laban has been doing to you. **13** I am the **God of Bethel** Ⓕ, where you poured oil on the stone marker and made a solemn vow to me. Get up, leave this land, and return to your native land.'" **14** Then Rachel and Leah answered him, "Do we have any portion or inheritance in our father's family? **15** Are we not regarded by him as outsiders? For he has sold us and has certainly spent our purchase price. **16** In fact, all the wealth that God has taken away from our father belongs to us and to our children. So do whatever God has said to you."

Passage Outline

Obedience Required
(Gen. 31:2-3)

Obedience Declared
(Gen. 31:4-13)

Obedience Affirmed
(Gen. 31:14-16)

Keywords

Ⓐ Laban couldn't hide his resentment of Jacob.

Ⓑ Canaan, where his father, Isaac, still lived (v. 18).

Ⓒ God's often-repeated promise. Jacob would have needed this word of assurance as he headed back toward Esau, who had threatened to kill him.

Ⓓ God is always at work in, through, and in spite of sinful actions to ensure that His plan is being accomplished (Gen. 50:20; Job 42:2).

Ⓔ Jacob used his unique approach to breeding sheep for some time before explaining that it was God's idea, revealed to him in a dream.

Ⓕ God referred to Himself as the God whom Jacob had experienced in a personal way.

❯ EXPLORE THE TEXT

Laban's displeasure with Jacob was written on his face. Laban had retained Jacob's services on terms exclusively determined by Jacob (see Gen. 30:31). Under the terms of the contract, Jacob's revenue soon outstripped Laban's profits. Consequently, Laban's sons feared losing their inheritance.

Following God's command to go back home wasn't as simple as it might sound. Jacob left many broken bridges when he left home, but God had promised to be with him.

When have you seen God demonstrate faithfulness in surprising ways?

> **BIBLE SKILL: Memorize a verse and apply it to a real-life situation.** >> Memorize Genesis 31:3 in your favorite Bible translation. Compare it to Genesis 26:3; Exodus 3:12; Deuteronomy 31:23; Joshua 1:5; 3:7; Judges 6:16; 1 Kings 11:38; and Isaiah 43:2. Notice that the promise in each verse was made in conjunction with either a task God had assigned or a time of trouble. Record a couple of sentences in a journal stating ways Genesis 31:3 can help you in a specific situation today.

After noticing Laban's attitude and hearing from God, Jacob met with his family far away from Laban's interference. Jacob explained his predicament by providing proof of Laban's trickery. Although he had tried pleasing Laban with hard work, Laban had repeatedly cheated him.

Jacob acknowledged that his prosperity wasn't the result of his understanding of animal husbandry; rather, God had blessed him. God divinely let Jacob know that He would bless him in spite of Laban's deceitful actions. Jacob told his wives that God was directing him to return to his native land.

> **KEY DOCTRINE: Stewardship** >> God is the source of all blessings, temporal and spiritual; we owe to Him all we have and all we are (see Deut. 8:17-18).

How do the ways Jacob honored God in these verses compare to the ways a person could honor God today?

Rachel and Leah were from the region of Haran and hadn't lived anywhere else. Jacob's announcement meant they would be uprooted from everything and everyone they knew in order to move to a foreign land. Together the sisters determined that in his marital negotiations their father had sold them like any other commodity. Rachel and Leah recognized God's plan and were committed to Jacob and his God. They agreed to do whatever God had told Jacob to do.

How did God's past faithfulness influence the decision Rachel and Leah made?

› APPLY THE TEXT

> › Believers can be thankful for God's promises when facing jealousy and hostility.

> › Knowing that God has their best interests in mind, believers can honor Him and His directions.

> › Based on God's past faithfulness, believers can take steps of faith.

From whom do you sense jealousy and hostility? What steps do you need to take to address those expressions?

What are you doing to honor God in your life? What can you do to honor Him to a greater degree? In what areas do you need to be more obedient in following His directions for your life?

Share with the group ways God has been faithful in the past. Discuss ways those past experiences give you confidence to take faithful action in the future. Record insights gained from the sharing and discussion.

❯ DAILY EXPLORATION

Day 1: Believers should always answer God's call.

Read Genesis 31:2-3, noting God's directions to Jacob.

If the phrase "If looks could kill" were ever true, Laban must have given Jacob that look. Jacob realized he was no longer welcome in his father-in-law's house. Laban now looked at him with resentment and regret.

By causing Jacon to notice that his in-laws were jealous of him, God began pricking Jacob's heart. Although circumstances by themselves aren't always accurate indicators of God's will, the Lord often uses difficult circumstances to make His children uncomfortable so that they'll follow Him. God reminded Jacob of His previous promise (see 28:15). Although Jacob had wanted to return home earlier, after working fourteen years for Rachel's hand in marriage, the timing wasn't right. Six years later, with Jacob's family and wealth firmly established, God would fulfill His promise.

Jacob had left many broken bridges when he left home. His brother had been so angry that he had threatened to kill him (see 27:41). His father had been so distressed over Jacob's dishonesty that he had trembled uncontrollably (see v. 33). How would his family receive him? Would his brother carry out his threat? Would his father accept him as a son? With so many unknowns, staying put would have been the easy choice. When God calls, staying put may seem like the safe choice, but answering His call is always the right decision.

How has God demonstrated His faithfulness in your life?

Day 2: God cares for His own.

Read Genesis 31:4-9, identifying God's continued provision for Jacob.

Jacob confidentially shared his plans with Rachel and Leah. He pointed out that the father of his wives had rejected him, while the God of his father had accepted him. Laban had made the mistake of basing his relationship with Jacob on opportunism and performance. God, the wise Father, unconditionally loves and cares for His own.

In spite of Laban's underhanded dealings, God turned the tables on him, preventing Jacob from being defrauded. Notice the change in Jacob's response to unfavorable circumstances. Earlier in his life he took matters into his own hands, but now he honestly evaluated the situation and made his family aware of the situation, showing tremendous spiritual growth.

When have you sensed God's guidance in making a difficult decision? How was this experience different from other decisions you've made?

Day 3: God blesses complete obedience.

Read Genesis 31:10-13, paying attention to the details of Jacob's dream.

The laws of heredity were unknown to humanity until the Austrian botanist Gregor Mendel conducted his experiments in the latter part of the nineteenth century. But God knew the laws of heredity from the beginning. He gave Jacob directions that enabled him to take advantage of those laws in breeding his flocks. God is the giver of life's blessings, and all believers would do well to give God glory as Jacob did.

As He had done before (see 28:10-15), God divinely let Jacob know that He would bless him in spite of Laban's deceitful actions. Notice Jacob's response. He immediately answered when God called. The presence and power of God come to believers when they declare their complete obedience to Him. They can't expect God to bless partial or conditional obedience, as King Saul learned when he kept the spoils of war for sacrifice (see 1 Sam. 15:14-23).

Jacob told his wives that God was directing him to return to his native land. No doubt Jacob had worried about the way his wives would respond. He loved his family, and he wanted them to remain with him. Would his wives follow him? Regardless of the way others respond, we must faithfully follow God's plan when He unveils it. We must never let others determine our obedience to God. In the end all believers will be judged according to their faithfulness to God.

How do the ways Jacob honored God in these verses compare to ways a person could honor God today?

Day 4: God provides our ultimate inheritance.

Read Genesis 31:14-15, considering Rachel and Leah's response.

Rachel and Leah concluded that they had no portion or inheritance in their father's family. When Jacob arrived, Laban had only daughters, meaning at the death of their father, the family inheritance would be split between them. Since then Laban had fathered several sons. The two sisters realized that their father had excluded them from any inheritance. Although they had worked in the family business, it would pass to their brothers. Having no inheritance, the sisters had been abandoned by their father.

Evidently, Laban had given his daughters the same disdainful look he gave Jacob. Their father treated them like outsiders, not like family. The Hebrew word translated *outsiders* can refer to a foreigner or a stranger. They may have first sensed the way their father felt about them at their weddings, when, instead of treating them like daughters, he used them for leverage to gain fourteen years of labor from Jacob.

Do you find Rachel and Leah's conclusions surprising? Would you make the same decision?

Day 5: God has a divine plan for every believer.

Read Genesis 31:16, underlining the end of the verse.

Rachel and Leah recognized God's divine plan. Although their father had treated them poorly, God had overridden their father's selfishness by providing for them. Instead of wallowing in self-pity, lamenting the fact that their father didn't love or care for them, they acknowledged God's providential care—a sign that they were trusting Jacob's God.

Rather than encouraging Jacob to pursue his plans, the sisters encouraged him to follow God's plans. Whatever the future held, Rachel and Leah put their lives and the lives of their children in God's hands. Jacob's heart must have jumped for joy when his own loved ones wholeheartedly and unreservedly endorsed his desire to do God's will. Rachel and Leah declared their allegiance to Jacob and his God, recognizing that God had used Jacob to provide them with a future.

How does God's past faithfulness influence the decisions you make?

The Holy Scriptures are our letters from home.

AUGUSTINE OF HIPPO

❯ OBEY THE TEXT

Reflect on the truths found in Genesis 31 and record your responses to the following questions or discuss them with two other members of your Bible-study group.

What reactions are common after making a life-altering decision, even when we know the decision is what God asked us to do?

When has "But God" (v. 7) been true of your life's circumstances?

How did Leah and Rachel express their faith in God? How do you express your faith in God?

MEMORIZE

The LORD said to him, "Go back to the land of your fathers and to your family, and I will be with you."
GENESIS 31:3

MY THOUGHTS

Record insights and questions from this session's group experience and daily exploration.

MY RESPONSE

Note specific ways you'll put into practice the truth explored this week.

MY PRAYERS

List specific prayer needs and answers to remember this week.

Transformed

God transforms people for use in His divine plan.

Genesis 32:24-32

Think about a time when you suffered a hardship. How did it affect you? How did you mature through that hardship?

We often view crises as unwanted intrusions in our lives, robbing us of joy and stealing our dreams. We feel cheated, thinking that life is unfair or that God doesn't care. We don't realize that God often orchestrates these unpleasant events for our good, to transform us into His image. More concerned for our good than our comfort, God puts us in positions where we can listen and learn.

❯ UNDERSTAND THE CONTEXT

After twenty years in exile, Jacob neared his homeland. Once he crossed the Jabbok River, he would enter the territory where Esau lived. To prepare to meet his brother, Jacob first sent messengers to Esau informing him of his plans. The messengers returned with news that Esau was leading four hundred men out to meet his brother (see Gen. 32:3-6).

The report of such a large number didn't bode well. Reasoning that Esau still begrudged his past behavior and planned to attack him, Jacob split his family and livestock into two groups (see vv. 7-8), hoping the slaughter of one group would appease Esau's thirst for vengeance. Then the defrauded twin brother might spare the other group.

Next Jacob prayed (see vv. 9-12). He identified God as the God of his father and grandfather, but Jacob's petition wasn't grounded in their relationships with God. Rather, he based it on his own experience with the Lord. He opened and closed the body of this prayer with God's previous pledges to him. Acknowledging his unworthiness of God's kindness and faithfulness, Jacob identified his progeny and prosperity as evidence of these characteristics of God. Then he petitioned God for deliverance from his brother's wrath.

After he prayed, Jacob took pragmatic steps to pacify his brother (see vv. 13-21). He separated animals from his flocks and herds to present as gifts to Esau. Then he designated servants to drive each type of animal in separate groups. As each group met Esau, the servant was to tell him the animals were a gift from Jacob.

Jacob's final preparation to meet Esau was unplanned. Initiated by God, it resulted in the final transformation of Jacob. Alone that night, Jacob met an unidentified man and wrestled with Him until dawn (see vv. 24-32). At daybreak the man changed Jacob's name to Israel.

❯ GENESIS 32:24-32

24 Jacob was left alone, and **a man** ⓐ wrestled with him until daybreak. **25** When the man saw that he could not defeat him, he struck Jacob's hip socket as they wrestled and dislocated his hip. **26** Then he said to Jacob, "Let me go, for it is **daybreak** ⓑ." But Jacob said, "I will not let you go unless you **bless me** ⓒ." **27** "What is your name?" **the man asked** ⓓ. "Jacob," he replied. **28** "Your name will no longer be Jacob," he said. "It will be Israel because you have struggled with God and **with men** ⓔ and have prevailed." **29** Then Jacob asked him, "Please tell me your name." But he answered, "**Why do you ask my name?** ⓕ" And he blessed him there. **30** Jacob then named the place Peniel, "For I have **seen God** ⓖ face to face," he said, "yet my life has been spared." **31** The sun shone on him as he passed by Penuel—limping because of his hip. **32** That is why, still today, the Israelites don't eat the thigh muscle that is at the hip socket: because he struck Jacob's hip socket at the thigh muscle.

Passage Outline

The Match (Gen. 32:24-26)

The Title (Gen. 32:27-29)

The Venue (Gen. 32:30-32)

Keywords

ⓐ The man is referred to as both an angel and God when this story is recounted in Hosea 12:3-4.

ⓑ When the sun came up, Jacob would be able to see his face.

ⓒ No one seeks a blessing from a subordinate. Jacob realized he was in the presence of a superior "man."

ⓓ The "man" no doubt knew whom he was wrestling. He wanted Jacob to confess who and what he was.

ⓔ Jacob had struggled with his father (27:1-29), his brother (v. 41), his uncle (29:25), and his cousins (31:1).

ⓕ No answer was given. On some level Jacob already knew with whom he had been wrestling.

ⓖ The expression "face to face" in reference to God isn't meant to be taken literally, because God is invisible (Col. 1:15; 1 Tim. 1:17).

> EXPLORE THE TEXT

Jacob had spent much of his life wrestling with people, such as Esau, Isaac, and Laban, and now God came to him in the form of a wrestler. Unlike most wrestling matches, which are divided into rounds, this match was one continuous fight that lasted until daybreak. Jacob doggedly held on with all of his might until the Lord ended the wrestling match by blessing Jacob. After wrestling with the Lord all night, Jacob discovered that he needed more than material wealth. He needed God and His transforming work in his life.

What keeps people from being desperate for God's blessing? How does an encounter with God foster a desire for His blessing?

From his wrestling match Jacob learned that the Lord wasn't finished with him yet. God gave him a new identity. Before God continued the transformation process in Jacob's life, He called for complete transparency from Jacob. Jacob would have to admit who he was and the condition of his heart.

What are the dangers of not confessing our past? How do honesty and humility open the door to spiritual transformation?

Throughout the Bible a person's name often identified his character, and the giving of a new name meant either a change in nature or a change in relationship. No longer would he be called Jacob ("he cheats" or "he supplants"); God named him Israel, meaning "he struggles with God" or "God rules." After Jacob had been broken and blessed by God, his destiny would forever change. Though transformation is a lifelong process, Jacob's transformation had begun with two steps. He had desperately sought God's blessing and submitted himself to the Lord in humility.

What does a surrendered life look like from God's perspective? What does a surrendered life look like from a human perspective?

Before Jacob wrestled with God, his world was dark, literally and figuratively. The next day the sun shone on him; it was a new day, a new beginning by God's design. Yet Jacob left with a limp, reminding him that God would always be with him.

What are some life markers for believers? How can believers memorialize their spiritual lessons so that they won't forget the insight gained?

> **BIBLE SKILL: Use other Scriptures to better understand the meaning and significance of biblical phrases and concepts.** >> Jacob named the place where he wrestled with an anonymous man Peniel, because he said, "I have seen God face to face" (Gen. 32:30). Other people in the Bible made similar statements. Read Genesis 16:1-13 and Isaiah 6 and identify the analogous statement in each passage. What insights into Jacob's experience do these two passages provide? What other Bible passages might help interpret Jacob's statement?

› APPLY THE TEXT

> › True transformation leads believers to value and seek God's blessing above all else.

> › When believers submit to God, transformation occurs.

> › Believers can establish life markers that remind them of critical spiritual insights gained in their walk with the Lord.

What steps do you need to take this week to more regularly place yourself in a position to encounter God? What barriers do you need to remove and how?

Review your spiritual journey, especially noting times when you experienced greater spiritual growth. What role did your willingness to submit to God play in those times? Take time to pray, asking God to help you grow in your willingness to submit to Him.

Spend time as a group sharing life-marker stories and the lessons learned. Discuss ways the group can help other believers establish life markers.

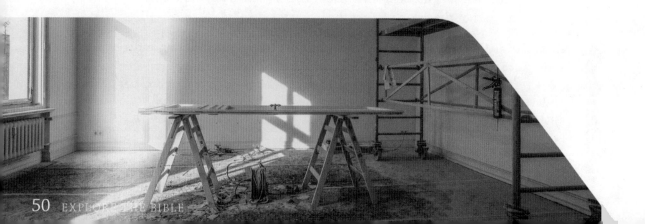

❯ DAILY EXPLORATION

Day 1: Believers should expect to wrestle with God at times in their lives.

Read Genesis 32:24-25, noting the length of the wrestling match.

Just as Jacob had met God during a lonely night in Bethel (see 28:10-22) after leaving behind an angry brother and a disappointed father, Jacob spent another lonely night with a surprising heavenly visitor. Some theologians believe the man who wrestled with Jacob is a preincarnate appearance of Christ. Although Scripture doesn't explicitly state the man's identity, it was clearly the Lord or one of His angels (see 32:30).

Jacob was in no mood for a wrestling match. He secretly escaped Haran so that Laban wouldn't confront him (see 31:20). Then he developed a plan to avoid fighting with his brother (see 32:3-8). The last thing on Jacob's mind was another conflict.

If Jacob's opponent was God or one of His representatives, why couldn't He defeat Jacob? Make no mistake about it; the Lord prevailed in the match by dislocating Jacob's hip and causing a permanent limp (see v. 31). Nevertheless, Jacob wouldn't give up. He doggedly held on with all his might until the Lord blessed him.

How does this passage characterize Jacob's life? What similarities do you see in your life?

Day 2: True transformation leads believers to seek God's blessings.

Read Genesis 32:26, considering Jacob's request for a blessing.

With the pain of a dislocated hip searing through Jacob's body, the wrestling match was effectively finished. All Jacob could do was hold on in spite of his suffering, pleading for a blessing from his heavenly visitor. Quitting wasn't part of Jacob's makeup. At Bethel God had promised Jacob His blessings. From a material perspective the promise was fulfilled because Jacob was wealthy with flocks, herds, and servants. After wrestling with the Lord all night, Jacob discovered that he needed more than material wealth. He needed God and His transforming work in his life. Jacob was unwilling to relinquish God's presence: "I will not let you go unless you bless me." True transformation leads believers to value and seek God's blessings above all else.

How have you experienced life change as a result of your faith in Christ? In what ways do you still need God to change you?

Day 3: Believers must be honest about their past.

Read Genesis 32:27, underlining Jacob's name.

The Hebrew name Jacob meant "deceiver" or "heel grabber," a reputation Jacob lived with most of his life. By asking Jacob to state his name, God forced Jacob to admit his true sinful nature. Before God continued the transformation process in Jacob's life, He called for complete transparency from Jacob. Jacob would have to admit who he was and the condition of his heart. God broke and then humbled Jacob so that he could reach his godly potential.

What He did for Jacob, God also does for believers today. If we're full of ourselves, pride, or sin or are bound by our past, we're unusable. As we humble ourselves and submit to God, He molds and shapes our lives.

What are the dangers of not confessing your past? How do honesty and humility open the door to spiritual transformation?

 KEY DOCTRINE: Salvation >> Regeneration, or the new birth, is a work of God's grace whereby believers become new creatures in Christ Jesus.

Day 4: Believers are changed by God's grace.

Read Genesis 32:28-29, underlining Jacob's new name, Israel.

Most of Jacob's life had been a struggle with men. He cheated his brother, deceived his blind father, and outwitted his unscrupulous uncle. Always looking for the upper hand, Jacob prevailed against men by trusting in his own schemes. Then he struggled with God, losing the match with a limp (see vv. 25,31) but gaining a victory when God transformed him.

Jacob's new name signified a new identity. He wasn't the same man who had left Canaan twenty years earlier (see 31:38). He would enter the land of blessing a changed man, now known as Israel. This new title would also become the name of God's people, the descendants of Jacob.

When believers encounter God and His transforming grace, they're forever changed. No matter how badly we've failed Him before, God can give us a new identity. Empowered from on high, we can find purpose and joy by serving the Lord.

After Jacob was broken and blessed by God, his destiny, as well as the destinies of those who followed him, would forever change. What was true for Jacob is still true today. When we submit to God, transformation occurs. Blessings follow people who make seeking Him their highest priority.

What does it look like for you to live a life surrendered to God?

Day 5: Believers should memorialize spiritual lessons in their lives.

Read Genesis 32:30-32, identifying the memorial Jacob created.

Recognizing that he had encountered the Lord, Jacob named the place of his wrestling match Peniel ("face of God") as a sense of awe and amazement swept over him. Having met God at Bethel (see 28:19) and Mahanaim (see 32:1-2), Jacob wanted to memorialize his third spiritual landmark. With each heavenly visitation Jacob renamed the meeting place, acknowledging God's presence and transformation in his life. God was preparing Jacob not only to meet Esau but also to become the father of the twelve tribes of Israel.

At Peniel God had spared Jacob. Jacob had thought seeing God face-to-face would bring death, but instead it brought him a changed life. By renaming the location and memorializing his encounter with God, Jacob associated Peniel with his spiritual transformation.

What are some life markers for you? How can you memorialize your spiritual lessons so that you won't forget the insight gained?

If we cannot be transformed, we will settle for being informed or conformed.

JOHN ORTBERG

❯ OBEY THE TEXT

Reflect on the truths found in Genesis 32 and record your responses to the following questions or discuss them with two other members of your Bible-study group.

What changes do you see in Jacob's life from these verses? What comparisons can you make to your life?

How can believers mature through difficult experiences?

How has God transformed your life? Share with the group at least one way God has produced visible change through your journey.

MEMORIZE

"Your name will no longer be Jacob," he said. "It will be Israel because you have struggled with God and with men and have prevailed."
GENESIS 32:28

MY THOUGHTS

Record insights and questions from this session's group experience and daily exploration.

_____

_____

_____

_____

_____

_____

_____

MY RESPONSE

Note specific ways you'll put into practice the truth explored this week.

_____

_____

_____

_____

_____

_____

_____

MY PRAYERS

List specific prayer needs and answers to remember this week.

_____

_____

_____

_____

_____

_____

_____

Reconciled

Reconciled relationships are a blessing from God, and the greatest blessing is a restored relationship with Him.

Genesis 33:1-15

What obstacles get in the way of reconciling a broken relationship? How can reconciling with others foster a person's spiritual growth?

Talking about reconciliation is easier than doing it. Whether from pride, fear of conflict, or fear of rejection, some people choose to allow a once healthy relationship to wither and die rather than face confrontation. They focus on what reconciliation might cost, ignoring what can be gained: a restored relationship, healing, forgiveness, and renewed love.

❯ UNDERSTAND THE CONTEXT

Genesis 33 presents the final confrontation between Jacob and Esau. The narrative breaks into three major segments.

1. The first segment (see vv. 1-4) describes the moment the two estranged brothers met after twenty years of separation.

2. The second segment (see vv. 5-15) records the two men's conversation on this occasion.

3. The third segment (see vv. 16-20) reports the geographical location where each brother settled afterward.

Jacob imagined the worst and planned accordingly. Seeing a large band of men rapidly approaching in the distance, he aligned his family in groups (see vv. 1-3). The two concubines went first. Leah and her children followed a short distance behind them. Jacob's beloved Rachel and her only child, Joseph, were in the rearmost position. Jacob stationed himself at the front of his caravan. Surprisingly, when Jacob met Esau, violence didn't erupt. Instead, Esau ran to embrace Jacob (see v. 4).

The conversation between the two brothers (see vv. 5-15) divides into two topics.

1. The first topic concerns the changes that had occurred during Jacob's twenty-year exile (see vv. 5-11). This portion of the conversation is likewise composed of two parts. First Jacob presented his family to his brother. Then he persuaded Esau to accept his gifts.

2. The second topic in their conversation focuses on the direction Jacob and his family would travel after this reunion (see vv. 12-15).

Jacob's relationship with God lessened his fear of Esau. If God had spared his life, wouldn't He also protect him from his brother? Jacob boldly testified to God's provision during the twenty years he had been absent. The value of his gift and the size of his family and herds confirmed his testimony. Jacob politely turned down his brother's offer of protection to travel to Seir. Instead, he migrated to Canaan and settled at Shechem.

❯ GENESIS 33:1-15

1 Now Jacob looked up and **saw Esau Ⓐ** coming toward him with four hundred men. So he divided the children among Leah, Rachel, and the two slave women. **2** He put the slaves and their children first, Leah and her children next, and **Rachel and Joseph last Ⓑ**. **3** He himself went on ahead and **bowed Ⓒ** to the ground **seven times Ⓓ** until he approached his brother. **4** But Esau ran to meet him, hugged him, threw his arms around him, and kissed him. Then they wept. **5** When Esau looked up and saw the women and children, he asked, "Who are these with you?" He answered, "The children God has **graciously Ⓔ** given your servant." **6** Then the slaves and their children approached him and bowed down. **7** Leah and her children also approached and bowed down, and then Joseph and Rachel approached and bowed down. **8** So Esau said, "**What do you mean Ⓕ** by this whole procession I met?" "To find favor with you, my lord," he answered. **9** "I have enough, my brother," Esau replied. "Keep what you have." **10** But Jacob said, "No, please! If I have found favor with you, take this gift from me. For indeed, I have seen your face, and it is like seeing God's face, since you have accepted me. **11** Please take my present that was brought to you, because God has been gracious to me and I have everything I need." So Jacob urged him until he accepted. **12** Then Esau said, "Let's move on, and I'll go ahead of you." **13** Jacob replied, "My lord knows that the children are weak, and I have nursing flocks and herds. If they are driven hard for one day, the whole herd will die. **14** Let my lord go ahead of his servant. I will continue on slowly, at a pace suited to the livestock and the children, until I come to my lord at Seir." **15** Esau said, "Let me leave some of my people with you." But he replied, "Why do that? Please indulge me, my lord."

Passage Outline

Put Aside Your Pride
(Gen. 33:1-4)

Be Genuine
(Gen. 33:5-11)

Agree on Limits
(Gen. 33:12-15)

Keywords

Ⓐ Jacob had sent messengers ahead of him to let Esau know he was coming (Gen. 32:3-5).

Ⓑ Closest to Jacob's heart, farthest from Esau's men.

Ⓒ A sign of humility, respect, contrition—and fear.

Ⓓ This number is used throughout the Bible to represent completeness.

Ⓔ Similar to *favor* in verses 8 and 10 After Jacob had experienced God's grace, he now hoped to receive Esau's grace. The most complete picture of grace is found in Jesus Christ (John 1:17), but grace is also an Old Testament concept (Gen. 6:8; Pss. 4:1; 51:1).

Ⓕ Perhaps he was being gracious, but Esau seemed to be completely clueless as to why Jacob would approach him with such humility and generosity.

> EXPLORE THE TEXT

When Jacob saw Esau coming toward him with four hundred men, he was afraid. Never without a plan, he quickly divided his family into three groups in case Esau's intentions were violent, giving his beloved wife Rachel and son Joseph an avenue of escape.

Unrestrained fear can make God's children do unhealthy things. How can believers overcome fear with faith?

In the face of imminent danger, Jacob faced Esau and his mighty band of warriors alone, demonstrating his trust in God. Clothed in humility, Jacob limped and bowed to the ground seven times before Esau as a sign of respect for his older brother. In a scene reminiscent of the father and the prodigal son, Esau ran toward Jacob.

What steps of preparation should a person take before seeking reconciliation, knowing that pride hurts and humility helps in building good relationships?

Jacob's answer to Esau's question proved that his life had genuinely changed. In a single sentence he testified of God's grace and of his transformation. As the three groups of wives and children caught up with Jacob, they too bowed before Esau as a sign of respect.

How do a group's actions reveal the true values of the person who influences them most?

Before Jacob met Esau, he sent 550 animals with servants as a gift for Esau (see Gen. 32:13-16). Once formal introductions were made, Esau asked about the parade of animals. Jacob explained that he was looking for grace, honoring Esau as the older sibling in accordance with the custom of that day. Deeply touched, Esau made a gracious statement that canceled all of Jacob's debt. In the end Esau wanted a restored relationship more than he wanted restitution for his stolen blessing.

What are some ways to demonstrate a genuine desire to reconcile a broken relationship?

Jacob stood before his brother exhausted from his nightlong wrestling match with the Lord. Assuming the role of the protective older brother, Esau graciously offered Jacob his assistance. As he had done earlier, Jacob declined the offer, telling Esau that he didn't want to burden or inconvenience him.

Throughout the conversation Jacob referred to God three times (see 33:5,10-11), while Esau never mentioned God at all. Sensing their differences, Jacob established boundaries so that no other unnecessary conflicts would erupt between the two brothers.

How important is agreeing on boundaries in a relationship? What types of boundaries are appropriate?

❯ APPLY THE TEXT

> ❯ True transformation is seen in approaching others with humility.

> ❯ Genuine reconciliation can occur only when both parties demonstrate a genuine desire to be restored.

> ❯ Creating wise safeguards can minimize future conflicts.

How can you cultivate true humility in your life? Ask God to help you take the steps needed to do so.

Identify relationships you need to mend. How can you restore them? What actions do you need to take?

What boundaries do you need to establish with others to minimize unhealthy conflict? What actions do you need to take to establish those boundaries? How can your Bible-study group help you establish and maintain those relational boundaries?

❯ DAILY EXPLORATION

Day 1: Believers can overcome fear with faith.

Read Genesis 33:1-2, noting Jacob's plan for his family.

Fresh from his encounter with God, Jacob faced his first test of faith. Providing opportunities for spiritual growth, tests often follow mountaintop experiences.

Jacob's hasty plan, hatched in fear, would have lifelong implications. By placing Joseph in a more secured position, Jacob unwittingly sparked the fire of contempt in the hearts of his other sons toward Joseph, culminating in attempted murder and eventual estrangement (see 37:18-28). The cycle of unguarded favoritism that destroyed Jacob's relationship with Esau now brooded in the hearts of his own sons.

In what areas of your life do you experience fear most? How can faith help you overcome those fears?

Day 2: Humility can help heal a broken relationship.

Read Genesis 33:3-4, identifying Esau's response to Jacob.

With such a show of force, Esau had carved out for himself position and power. He was no longer the weaker brother, whining over a lost blessing. He now commanded his own army. If Esau had wanted to make good on his threat, killing Jacob would have been a small feat. Clothed in humility, Jacob limped and bowed to the ground seven times before Esau as a sign of respect for his older brother.

Esau couldn't control his emotions as he threw his arms around Jacob and kissed him. Love and forgiveness saturated their reunion. Neither was the same selfish man who grew up despising the other. The past was forgotten as Esau embraced Jacob in a gesture of acceptance.

Jacob's reconciliation with Esau was the result of his previous meetings with God (see 32:1-2, 24-31). Only after being reconciled with God could Jacob be reconciled with Esau. During that pivotal wrestling match, God broke, humbled, and transformed Jacob. By first meeting with God, we can be ready to meet with others, regardless of how difficult the journey ahead may be.

What steps of preparation should you take before seeking reconciliation, knowing that pride hurts and humility helps in building good relationships?

KEY DOCTRINE: **Peace and war** >> It's the duty of Christians to seek peace with all people on principles of righteousness (see Rom. 12:18-19).

Day 3: Jesus has an impact on believers' lives.

Read Genesis 33:5-7, considering Esau's question.

Placing himself in a position of servitude before his older brother, Jacob acknowledged that God had blessed him with a large family in spite of all his shortcomings. Without knowing about Jacob's experience at Bethel or Mahanaim, Esau must have found those words strange because his only memories of Jacob were acts of selfishness and arrogance. But Jacob wasn't the same man; this was Israel.

Jacob's spiritual leadership had affected not only his older brother but also his servants, children, and wives as they followed in his footsteps. After encountering God, Jacob demonstrated that he was a changed man by the way he talked and lived, influencing the behavior of others. Similarly, when believers today spend time with Jesus, He will have a positive impact on the people around us.

How do your actions reveal the true values of the person who influences you most?

Day 4: Believers must seek God's guidance in reconciling with others.

Read Genesis 33:8-11, paying close attention to verse 11.

Jacob insisted that Esau accept his gift as a token indicating that all was forgiven. At first he called it a gift, meaning "an offering," as in a peace offering for all he had stolen from Esau when they were younger. After Esau's persistent reluctance Jacob called it a present, meaning "a blessing."

Jacob let Esau know that his gesture wasn't motivated by selfishness but was prompted by the gracious act of God, who had changed his life and supplied all his needs. While Esau never mentioned God in the entire conversation, he was won over by the apparent change in Jacob's life. Finally, the past was permanently in the past.

Jacob took the first step with God's help, and Esau reciprocated. To have meaningful relationships, we must seek God's guidance and take the initiative by faith. We must also resist sweeping the conflict under the rug. Problems never go away; they multiply.

What are some ways to demonstrate a genuine desire to reconcile a broken relationship?

Day 5: God fulfills His promises.

Read Genesis 33:12-15, considering Jacob's journey.

Evidently, both men assumed Jacob would spend time at Esau's home in Seir (Edom), but God took Jacob in a different direction—Succoth, where he built his home, free from fear of retaliation from Esau (see v. 17).

After living a few years in Succoth, Jacob crossed the Jordan River and arrived at Shechem. There he built an altar to God, calling it "God, the God of Israel" or "powerful is the God of Israel" as a public testimony that the God of his grandfather, Abraham, and his father, Isaac, was also his God (see v. 20). The journey to Canaan was now complete. God had fulfilled His promise.

When have you seen God fulfill a promise in your life? How did you respond to His faithfulness?

> BIBLE SKILL: **Use a Bible atlas and a Bible dictionary to locate and learn about places mentioned in Scripture.** >> Find the locations of Seir, Succoth, Shechem, and the Jabbok River in a Bible atlas. Then use a Bible dictionary to learn more about each location. Trace Jacob's travel in Genesis 33.

Never ruin an apology with an excuse.

KIMBERLY JOHNSON

❯ OBEY THE TEXT

Reflect on the truths found in Genesis 33 and record your responses to the following questions or discuss them with two other members of your Bible-study group.

How is Esau's reaction in the story surprising? When have you experienced a similar reaction to a circumstance in a broken relationship?

How can Christians show godly contentment in their lives—in relationships, finances, health struggles, and so forth?

Why is forgiveness challenging, whether you're seeking or offering it? How can you offer forgiveness when you've been deeply hurt?

MEMORIZE

"Please take my present that was brought to you, because
   God has been gracious to me and I have everything
   I need." So Jacob urged him until he accepted.

GENESIS 33:11

MY THOUGHTS

Record insights and questions from this session's group experience and daily exploration.

MY RESPONSE

Note specific ways you'll put into practice the truth explored this week.

MY PRAYERS

List specific prayer needs and answers to remember this week.

LEADER GUIDE—SESSION 1

> ## GETTING STARTED

OPENING OPTIONS: Choose one of the following to open the group discussion.

WEEKLY QUOTATION DISCUSSION STARTER: "To lie a little is not possible; whoever lies, lies a whole lie."—Victor Hugo

> How does this quotation apply to your experiences?

> What are some situations in which we're tempted "to lie a little"?

One reason we often feel comfortable telling "small" lies is that we believe they'll carry smaller consequences, if any. As Jacob discovered, however, all lies have consequences, and those consequences often take us down roads we never intended to travel.

CREATIVE ACTIVITY: Start the session by reenacting the scene between Isaac and Jacob. Blindfold one volunteer. Then have two or three other volunteers approach the blindfolded person one by one and say, "I have done as you told me. Please sit up and eat some of my game so that you may bless me." Encourage the volunteers to disguise their voices. Challenge the blindfolded volunteer to identify the people who speak.

> What situations might tempt you to deceive someone?

> Do any circumstances exist in which deceiving someone might be appropriate?

> ## UNDERSTAND THE CONTEXT

PROVIDE BACKGROUND: Briefly introduce members to Genesis 27–33, pointing out major themes, information, and ideas that will help them understand Genesis 27:18-29 (see pp. 5 and 7). Then, to help people personally connect today's context with the original context, use the following questions and statements.

> In the ancient world a firstborn son was expected to replace his father as the leader of his family. This responsibility also carried a reward in the form of a double portion of blessing, or inheritance. Jacob seems to have coveted both the responsibility and the blessing.

> Obvious divisions, tensions, and conflicts were present in Jacob's family. When you were growing up, how did your family typically handle tension and strife?

❯ EXPLORE THE TEXT

READ THE BIBLE: Ask a volunteer to read Genesis 27:18-29.

DISCUSS: Use the following questions to discuss group members' initial reactions to the text.

> What immediately stands out to you in this text as a theme or primary point?

> What do you find encouraging, timely, or convicting?

> Which part of Jacob's deception seems most disturbing to you? Why?

> If you were in Jacob's shoes, what emotions would you have experienced in that moment?

> What's your initial reaction to Isaac's blessing in verses 27-29?

> What are the implications of Jacob's receiving the blessing instead of Esau?

> How did Jacob's actions in these verses display a distrust of God?

> What else does this text teach us about God? About ourselves?

> What other questions or observations do you have?

NOTE: Provide ample time for group members to share responses and questions about the text. Don't feel pressured to prioritize the printed agenda over group members' personal experiences. If time allows, discuss responses to the questions in the personal reading.

❯ OBEY THE TEXT

RESPOND: Foster an environment of openness and action. Help individuals apply biblical truth to specific areas of personal thought, attitude, and/or behavior.

> What behaviors or circumstances have caused you to act deceitfully in the past?

> Who has permission to tell you when you're being selfish?

> What are some ways you can actively cultivate honesty and integrity this week?

> What are some ways you can actively trust God this week?

PRAY: Declare your agreement with God's Word, which teaches that lies and deception are destructive not only in your life but also in the lives of others. Express your desire to display honesty and integrity as a servant of God's kingdom in your church and community.

❯ GETTING STARTED

OPENING OPTIONS: Choose one of the following to open the group discussion.

WEEKLY QUOTATION DISCUSSION STARTER: "The place God calls you to is the place where your deep gladness and the world's deep hunger meet."—Frederick Buechner

> ❯ What's a source of "deep gladness" for you?

> ❯ In what directions have you sensed God leading you in recent years?

Jacob was a young man who made a lot of mistakes. Thankfully, God is able to use the consequences of our mistakes to guide us toward deeper encounters with Him.

CREATIVE ACTIVITY: Offer the visual learners and creative types in your group an opportunity to shine. Provide paper and crayons or markers for each person. Encourage everyone to sketch or draw the dream Jacob experienced in Genesis 28:12-15. After four or five minutes, allow volunteers to share their work.

> ❯ Which element in the dream do you like best? Why?

> ❯ What elements in other people's drawings do you enjoy?

❯ UNDERSTAND THE CONTEXT

PROVIDE BACKGROUND: Briefly introduce members to major themes, information, and ideas that will help them understand Genesis 28:10-22 (see p. 17). Then, to help people personally connect today's context with the original context, use the following questions and statements.

> ❯ Jacob's deceitful plan to receive his brother's blessing brought about several unintended consequences. For example, he never saw his mother or father again after he left for Haran. What were some other immediate and long-term consequences of Jacob's actions?

> ❯ Jacob's encounter with God in Genesis 28 is often viewed as surprising, given Jacob's deceitfulness in earlier chapters. What are some ways churches can intentionally be open and welcoming to those who, like Jacob, need to experience God's grace?

❯ EXPLORE THE TEXT

READ THE BIBLE: Ask a volunteer to read Genesis 28:10-22.

DISCUSS: Use the following questions to discuss group members' initial reactions to the text.

> What immediately stands out to you in this text as a theme or primary point?

> What do you find encouraging, timely, or convicting?

> What's your first impression of Jacob's dream?

> What specific promises did Jacob receive from God?

> When have you encountered God in a totally unexpected way?

> Was it right for Jacob to say he would follow God if God blessed him in specific ways? Explain.

> What specific promises did Jacob make to God?

> What else does this text teach us about God? About ourselves?

> What other questions or observations do you have?

NOTE: Provide ample time for group members to share responses and questions about the text. Don't feel pressured to prioritize the printed agenda over group members' personal experiences. If time allows, discuss responses to the questions in the personal reading.

❯ OBEY THE TEXT

RESPOND: Foster an environment of openness and action. Help individuals apply biblical truth to specific areas of personal thought, attitude, and/or behavior.

> What are some ways you can intentionally seek God's presence?

> Which of Jacob's promises to God can His followers apply today?

> How are you currently celebrating or commemorating spiritual milestones from your past?

> How can your church or group celebrate spiritual milestones from the past?

PRAY: Praise God for His willingness to make Himself known to you and the members of your group. Express your desire to spend time in God's presence and to grow in your connection with Him each day.

❯ GETTING STARTED

OPENING OPTIONS: Choose one of the following to open the group discussion.

WEEKLY QUOTATION DISCUSSION STARTER: "I sometimes wonder whether the church needs new members one-half as much as she needs the old bunch made over."—Billy Sunday

> How well has the church in general lived up to your expectations?

> In what ways have you felt the pressure of expectations as a church member?

It's worth repeating over and over again that the church should be a place where imperfect people feel welcome. There are no perfect people—only sinners saved by grace.

CREATIVE ACTIVITY: To connect with the romantic side of Jacob and Rachel's story, encourage group members to share their favorite romantic stories. Use the following questions to guide the discussion.

> What do you like best about the idealized relationships in movies and on TV?

> What irritates you about the idealized relationships in movies and on TV?

❯ UNDERSTAND THE CONTEXT

PROVIDE BACKGROUND: Briefly introduce members to major themes, information, and ideas that will help them understand Genesis 29:16-30 (see p. 27). Then, to help people personally connect today's context with the original context, use the following questions and statements.

> Jacob had a life-changing encounter with God at the well he named Bethel. That change was evident in his behavior at a different well, where he met his future wife. How do the images of a well and water serve as powerful symbols in Jacob's story?

> One key theme of Jacob's life and family is that God is comfortable using imperfect people to accomplish His plans. How have you seen that principle at work in your life?

❯ EXPLORE THE TEXT

READ THE BIBLE: Ask a volunteer to read Genesis 29:16-30.

DISCUSS: Use the following questions to discuss group members' initial reactions to the text.

> What immediately stands out to you in this text as a theme or primary point?

> What do you find encouraging, timely, or convicting?

> What evidence do you see in these verses that Jacob had been changed by his encounter with God at Bethel?

> Whom do you feel most sympathetic toward in these verses? Why?

> Whom do you feel most angry with in these verses? Why?

> What were some positive interactions and outcomes in this story?

> How do you typically respond when you feel deceived?

> What else does this text teach us about God? About ourselves?

> What other questions or observations do you have?

NOTE: Provide ample time for group members to share responses and questions about the text. Don't feel pressured to prioritize the printed agenda over group members' personal experiences. If time allows, discuss responses to the questions in the personal reading.

❯ OBEY THE TEXT

RESPOND: Foster an environment of openness and action. Help individuals apply biblical truth to specific areas of personal thought, attitude, and/or behavior.

> What's the right or godly way to respond when you've been deceived?

> How is God currently using imperfect people to teach you something important?

> What goals are you currently working hard to achieve?

> What steps can you take to ensure that your goals align with God's plan for your life?

PRAY: Thank God for the blessings you've received from your family. Praise Him for His ability to work in and through imperfect people, including yourself and your group members, to achieve His will and accomplish His plans.

❯ GETTING STARTED

OPENING OPTIONS: Choose one of the following to open the group discussion.

WEEKLY QUOTATION DISCUSSION STARTER: "The Holy Scriptures are our letters from home." —Augustine of Hippo

> ❯ What images or emotions come to mind when you hear the word *home?*

> ❯ When have you experienced a strong reminder that this world isn't your true home?

The concept of home can be both bitter and sweet—sometimes even in the same memory. In those moments it's helpful to remember that nothing we've yet experienced will compare with the joy of truly coming home to heaven.

CREATIVE ACTIVITY: Ask group members to determine the distance between your meeting room and the place they considered home when they were growing up. Encourage them to use mapping apps on their devices to be as exact as possible. Give small prizes to the person who's closest to home and to the person who's farthest away.

> ❯ When was the last time you visited this home?

> ❯ What emotions do you experience when you visit?

❯ UNDERSTAND THE CONTEXT

PROVIDE BACKGROUND: Briefly introduce members to major themes, information, and ideas that will help them understand Genesis 31:2-16 (see p. 37). Then, to help people personally connect today's context with the original context, use the following questions and statements.

> ❯ On his journey to Haran, Jacob had encountered God at Bethel. During that encounter God had promised Jacob a land of his own—a home for his people. After twenty years as a foreigner, Jacob longed to receive that promise.

> ❯ It's important to note that Jacob believed the promises he had received from God. He demonstrated faith by choosing to leave a stable situation and go to a new place. Which of God's promises are you currently counting on and working to receive?

❯ EXPLORE THE TEXT

READ THE BIBLE: Ask a volunteer to read Genesis 31:2-16.

DISCUSS: Use the following questions to discuss group members' initial reactions to the text.

> What immediately stands out to you in this text as a theme or primary point?

> What do you find encouraging, timely, or convicting?

> What specifically did God want Jacob to do?

> What risks were involved for Jacob and his family if they obeyed God?

> What did Jacob do well in these verses?

> How has God demonstrated His care and provision in your life?

> How would you describe the attitudes of Rachel and Leah?

> What else does this text teach us about God? About ourselves?

> What other questions or observations do you have?

NOTE: Provide ample time for group members to share responses and questions about the text. Don't feel pressured to prioritize the printed agenda over group members' personal experiences. If time allows, discuss responses to the questions in the personal reading.

❯ OBEY THE TEXT

RESPOND: Foster an environment of openness and action. Help individuals apply biblical truth to specific areas of personal thought, attitude, and/or behavior.

> In what ways are you currently seeking God's guidance and direction?

> How do you typically thank God for His provision in your life?

> Who taught you how to be a spiritual leader?

> In what areas would you like to grow as a spiritual leader in your family?

PRAY: Affirm your belief that God keeps His promises. Thank Him for the gifts you've received in and through your earthly home. Praise Him for the truth that countless blessings are waiting for you in your heavenly home.

❯ GETTING STARTED

OPENING OPTIONS: Choose one of the following to open the group discussion.

WEEKLY QUOTATION DISCUSSION STARTER: "If we cannot be transformed, we will settle for being informed or conformed."—John Ortberg

> ❯ What's your initial reaction to this quotation? Why?

> ❯ In what ways does our culture cater to and promote settling for being informed or conformed?

We place ourselves in danger when we believe that transformation is a passive process—that we sit back and let it happen to us. As Jacob discovered, genuine change usually takes a lot of work on our part.

CREATIVE ACTIVITY: Help group members connect with the action in this session's Scripture by asking a few volunteers to arm-wrestle each other. If you have enough volunteers, you can hold a brief tournament, awarding a small prize to the winner.

> ❯ How do you feel when you're getting ready to compete against someone? Why?

> ❯ What contests or competitions have driven you to make changes in your life?

❯ UNDERSTAND THE CONTEXT

PROVIDE BACKGROUND: Briefly introduce members to major themes, information, and ideas that will help them understand Genesis 32:24-32 (see p. 47). Then, to help people personally connect today's context with the original context, use the following questions and statements.

> ❯ Jacob had managed a huge undertaking in bringing all of his household possessions, flocks, herds, and family members from Haran to Canaan. However, one obstacle lay in his path: Esau. Jacob still needed to address the consequences of having deceived his brother more than twenty years earlier. What steps would you have taken to overcome that obstacle if you had been in Jacob's place?

> ❯ The Jacob who returned to Canaan wasn't the same man who had fled from his brother in fear for his life. Jacob had been changed, and he was about to receive a new name from God. How does God create change and growth in His children today?

❯ EXPLORE THE TEXT

READ THE BIBLE: Ask a volunteer to read Genesis 32:24-32.

DISCUSS: Use the following questions to discuss group members' initial reactions to the text.

- ❯ What immediately stands out to you in this text as a theme or primary point?

- ❯ What do you find encouraging, timely, or convicting?

- ❯ How can we confirm the identity of the man who wrestled Jacob?

- ❯ What does the image of wrestling communicate? How should we understand this contest between Jacob and God?

- ❯ Do you think Jacob acted appropriately in this situation? Explain.

- ❯ When have you wrestled with God or had difficulty submitting to Him?

- ❯ What's an experience that changed you in a profound way?

- ❯ What else does this text teach us about God? About ourselves?

- ❯ What other questions or observations do you have?

NOTE: Provide ample time for group members to share responses and questions about the text. Don't feel pressured to prioritize the printed agenda over group members' personal experiences. If time allows, discuss responses to the questions in the personal reading.

❯ OBEY THE TEXT

RESPOND: Foster an environment of openness and action. Help individuals apply biblical truth to specific areas of personal thought, attitude, and/or behavior.

- ❯ What obstacles currently stand between you and a deeper experience with God?

- ❯ In what area of spiritual growth would you like to experience a leap in progress?

- ❯ What steps can you take this week to seek a new blessing from God?

PRAY: Conclude the session by praising God for the ways He has led you and your group members to experience transformation. Express your desire to know Him better and to encounter Him more deeply each day.

> ## GETTING STARTED

OPENING OPTIONS: Choose one of the following to open the group discussion.

WEEKLY QUOTATION DISCUSSION STARTER: "Never ruin an apology with an excuse."
—Kimberly Johnson

> › When have you seen the truth of this statement in action?

> › What are some key ingredients of a good apology?

Most people have a hard time apologizing, in part because they have a hard time admitting that they were wrong. Fortunately for Jacob, he didn't carry that sentiment into his meeting with Esau.

CREATIVE ACTIVITY: Practice makes perfect, so offer your group members a chance to practice saying they're sorry. Ask volunteers to indicate how they would apologize in the following situations.

> › You accidentally bump into another car in a parking lot, causing a visible dent.

> › You write an email criticizing one of your coworkers but accidentally copy that person in the email.

> › You schedule a time to meet with a friend who needs advice. When the time for the meeting comes, you don't feel like going, so you don't show up.

> ## UNDERSTAND THE CONTEXT

PROVIDE BACKGROUND: Briefly introduce members to major themes, information, and ideas that will help them understand Genesis 33:1-15 (see p. 57). Then, to help people personally connect today's context with the original context, use the following questions and statements.

> › Twenty years passed between the time Jacob fled from Esau's wrath and the day he returned to Canaan with his new family. Jacob's actions before the meeting made it clear that he still feared his brother; nevertheless, he wanted reconciliation. What steps would you have taken to plan for the worst if you had been in Jacob's shoes?

> › Reconciling with someone who has hated you is a difficult process under any circumstances, but it's especially difficult when you know you were wrong. How hard do you find it to apologize for your mistakes?

❯ EXPLORE THE TEXT

READ THE BIBLE: Ask a volunteer to read Genesis 33:1-15.

DISCUSS: Use the following questions to discuss group members' initial reactions to the text.

> What immediately stands out to you in this text as a theme or primary point?

> What do you find encouraging, timely, or convicting?

> What do you like best about this scene? Why?

> What was Jacob's purpose in dividing his household into separate groups?

> How did Jacob show leadership in these verses?

> How did Jacob show repentance and respect in these verses?

> Why is it significant that Jacob equated seeing Esau with "seeing God's face" (v. 10)?

> What else does this text teach us about God? About ourselves?

> What other questions or observations do you have?

NOTE: Provide ample time for group members to share responses and questions about the text. Don't feel pressured to prioritize the printed agenda over group members' personal experiences. If time allows, discuss responses to the questions in the personal reading.

❯ OBEY THE TEXT

RESPOND: Foster an environment of openness and action. Help individuals apply biblical truth to specific areas of personal thought, attitude, and/or behavior.

> How can we determine when reconciliation is necessary in an important relationship?

> How can we determine when we should take the first step toward reconciliation?

> What are some obstacles that typically hinder you from apologizing when necessary?

> What's one step you need to take this week in order to follow Jacob's example?

PRAY: Confess your understanding that you've been forgiven of an unpayable debt through Jesus' death on the cross. Express your desire to forgive others and seek reconciliation because you've been forgiven.

TIPS FOR LEADING A GROUP

PRAYERFULLY PREPARE

Prepare for each session by—

> **reviewing the weekly material and group questions ahead of time;**

> **praying for each person in the group.**

Ask the Holy Spirit to work through you and the group discussion to help people take steps toward Jesus each week as directed by God's Word.

MINIMIZE DISTRACTIONS

Create a comfortable environment. If group members are uncomfortable, they'll be distracted and therefore not engaged in the group experience. Plan ahead by taking into consideration—

> **seating;**

> **temperature;**

> **lighting;**

> **food or drink;**

> **surrounding noise;**

> **general cleanliness (put pets away if meeting in a home).**

At best, thoughtfulness and hospitality show guests and group members they're welcome and valued in whatever environment you choose to gather. At worst, people may never notice your effort, but they're also not distracted. Do everything in your ability to help people focus on what's most important: connecting with God, with the Bible, and with others.

INCLUDE OTHERS

Your goal is to foster a community in which people are welcome just as they are but encouraged to grow spiritually. Always be aware of opportunities to—

> **invite** new people to join your group;

> **include** any people who visit the group.

An inexpensive way to make first-time guests feel welcome or to invite people to get involved is to give them their own copies of this Bible-study book.

ENCOURAGE DISCUSSION

A good small group has the following characteristics.

> **Everyone participates.** Encourage everyone to ask questions, share responses, or read aloud.

> **No one dominates—not even the leader.** Be sure what you say takes up less than half of your time together as a group. Politely redirect discussion if anyone dominates.

> **Nobody is rushed through questions.** Don't feel that a moment of silence is a bad thing. People often need time to think about their responses to questions they've just heard or to gain courage to share what God is stirring in their hearts.

> **Input is affirmed and followed up.** Make sure you point out something true or helpful in a response. Don't just move on. Build personal connections with follow-up questions, asking how other people have experienced similar things or how a truth has shaped their understanding of God and the Scripture you're studying. People are less likely to speak up if they fear that you don't actually want to hear their answers or that you're looking for only a certain answer.

> **God and His Word are central.** Opinions and experiences can be helpful, but God has given us the truth. Trust Scripture to be the authority and God's Spirit to work in people's lives. You can't change anyone, but God can. Continually point people to the Word and to active steps of faith.

KEEP CONNECTING

Think of ways to connect with members during the week. Participation during the session is always improved when members spend time connecting with one another away from the session. The more people are comfortable with and involved in one another's lives, the more they'll look forward to being together. When people move beyond being friendly and in the same group to truly being friends who form a community, they come to each session eager to engage instead of merely attending.

Encourage group members with thoughts, commitments, or questions from the session by connecting through—

> emails;
> texts;
> social media.

When possible, build deeper friendships by planning or spontaneously inviting group members to join you outside your regularly scheduled group time for—

> meals;
> fun activities;
> projects around your home, church, or community.

GROUP CONTACT INFORMATION

Name _____ Number _____
Email/social media _____

Name _____ Number _____
Email/social media _____

Name _____ Number _____
Email/social media _____

Name _____ Number _____
Email/social media _____

Name _____ Number _____
Email/social media _____

Name _____ Number _____
Email/social media _____

Name _____ Number _____
Email/social media _____

Name _____ Number _____
Email/social media _____

Name _____ Number _____
Email/social media _____

Name _____ Number _____
Email/social media _____

Name _____ Number _____
Email/social media _____